# Guide *to* DEVELOPING *a* LIBRARY MUSIC COLLECTION

## R. MICHAEL FLING

Collection Management &
Development Section
Association for Library Collections
& TechnicalServices

AMERICAN LIBRARY ASSOCIATION
Chicago   2008

# ALCTS Collection Management and Development Guides

ALCTS Publishing
50 E. Huron St.
Chicago, IL 60611
www.ala.org/alcts

ISBN 978-0-8389-8482-6

**Library of Congress Cataloging-in-Publication Data**

Fling, Robert Michael, 1941-
  Guide to developing a library music collection / R. Michael Fling.
    p. cm. -- (ALCTS collection management and development guides ; no. 14)
  Includes index.
  ISBN 978-0-8389-8482-6
  1. Music libraries--Collection development  I. Title.
  ML111.F46 2008
  025.2'18678--dc22
                          2008032558


Published and printed in the United States of America.

12  11  10  09  –08–  1  2  3  4

# CONTENTS

CONTENTS

# CONTENTS

# *INTRODUCTION*

Although the diverse communities and cultures of the world today face a myriad of conflicts and difficulties, music continues to have a near-global appeal and the study of music has become an important means of communication. Although a few intolerant societies have sought to restrict music, even to prohibit it altogether (the Puritans in seventeenth-century England and America, the Taliban in twentieth-century Afghanistan, to name just two), it is ubiquitous in our lives today. One has only to consider the number of health-club members using music to ease them through their treadmill routines, the variety of music-to-shop-by programs droning their undertones at the mall, and the music that provokes viewers' emotions in film and television.

"Music" has had different meanings for different people in different times, cultures, and contexts. [1] In the Middle Ages, music was a topic of metaphysical discourse and mystical speculation by learned university men (*musica speculativa*). To Shakespeare and Ben Johnson, it often meant a person—a performer—as even today it identifies a company bugler in the U.S. military. In seventeenth-century England, it could refer to a band of highwaymen! And, since at least that time, it has stood also for a physical object—the written or printed notes of a musical composition. To the students and faculty at a university music school, it is a form of high art, for many years created chiefly by dead, white, European men ("classical" or "serious" music). By the general public, it is typically regarded as entertainment on top-40s radio, purchased in compact-disc form at a "music store," or downloaded over the Internet.

While music may be the most widely experienced and appreciated of the arts, its technical language renders it one of the most obscure when it is written down, described, analyzed, and cataloged. The implications for libraries are considerable. It is widely acknowledged that extensive formal training in music is required to perform all but the most routine tasks in a library's music collections, and it is safe to say that virtually all music librarians practicing today studied music formally and sang or played an instrument before becoming library professionals. In its brochure "Music Librarianship—Is It for You?" the Music Library Association (MLA) states that "Training in music must be the equivalent of at least substantial under-graduate work. . . . Because music librarians need a thorough knowledge of music history and repertory, a second master's degree in music is required or highly desired for some positions." [2]

Unfortunately, some library administrators have the view that all librarians rolled off a "Library School, Inc." assembly line and that they must therefore be interchangeable, like the fenders of Ford's Model T. At least one distinguished non-music library administrator has declared, however, that music librarians *are* a special breed: Michael Gorman, a past president of the American Library Association, wrote that "music librarians live all aspects of their lives with a musical accompaniment; their private and working lives are marinated in music, and that is what makes them different from [other librarians]." [3] While it is not inconceivable that a librarian without formal musical training could acquire the skills to develop a music collection, such a librarian would have a much tougher row to hoe than will one who is musically informed. [4]

The novice music selector who is feeling overwhelmed by the prospect of doing this work might at this point consider skipping momentarily ahead to the chapter on "Selection Strategies" for some reassurances that "Though this be madness, yet there is method in it" (Shakespeare's *Hamlet*, act 2, scene 2). That chapter includes discussion of music collection policies, a summary of basic collection-building objectives, strategies for keeping current with the music world, and some thoughts about music approval plans.

Strategies for keeping up with new publications are discussed in the chapters on the various publication formats. In addition, the concluding chapter, "Getting Help," demonstrates that when a music collection development coach is not close at hand to help when you get stuck, there are many online and print sources to turn to. You need not be as isolated and resource-deprived as were Crusoe, the Swiss Robinsons, and Piggy and Ralph.

# Music in Libraries

The study of music relies on the interrelated use of three distinct information formats: books and journals (words), which communicate intellectual discourse about the art; recordings (sounds, and more recently, visuals), which preserve and disseminate particular musical performances; and printed and manuscript music (notes), which transmit the composer's intentions to the performer and scholar, and which the librarian who acquires and interprets the music to library users must be able to read.

Resources in all of these formats have been collected by libraries in academic institutions, including conservatories of music, and by public libraries. Collecting emphasis has traditionally been on music of European-influenced Western cultures, commonly referred to as "classical" music. However, collections have expanded to include popular, ethnic, and folk musics as public interest in those genres grew and they became part of academic curricula. Various special libraries and archives also collect and preserve music in whatever genres and formats suit their particular missions.

The peculiarities of music formats, and of their acquisition, binding, shelving, circulation, and cataloging, have meant that many academic music collections function as separate entities, whether as discrete "branch" libraries, typically housed within the school of music, or as music departments within general libraries. These music collections are used not just by scholars, but also by instrumentalists, singers, and conductors. For example, someone preparing a work for performance might consult background literature for historical insights, read treatises on performance practice for historically accurate interpretation of works of earlier times, study analyses of the work's formal structure, listen to performances recorded by others, compare multiple editions to evaluate various editors' interpretations, consult critical editions for the most accurate versions of the music according to current scholarship, and examine facsimiles of manuscripts to see the work in the composer's own hand.

Outside the academic realm, public libraries collect in support of self-education and recreation. Their music collections vary widely depending upon the size of the population served, economic conditions and funding levels, the presence of particular ethnic communities, the success of school music programs, and other local factors—and some public libraries collect no music at all.[5] Public book and periodical collections tend to reflect increased publication about, and interest in, popular music, electronic music, music of ethnic minorities, women's music, and the music business. Sound recordings are the backbone of most public library music collections, with classical music, opera, musicals, blues, and world music among the most popular genres. In some libraries, lack of in-house musical expertise causes librarians to rely solely on patron requests for what to purchase. Printed music—if collected at all—is typically limited to easy popular and film-music anthologies for piano, guitar, and a few band instruments.

Specialized music collections are found at historical societies; research institutes; museums; the archives of composers, publishers, cathedrals, and monasteries; orchestras, opera companies, and other performing organizations. They can also be found at broadcast stations and national libraries and music centers.

## EUROPEAN ANTECEDENTS

The relevance of music to library collections was recognized early on in Europe. For centuries, royal houses and ecclesiastical establishments acquired music in support of aristocratic entertainments and religious and civic ceremonies, though the concept of "public" music collections did not arise until the French Revolution. In 1795, the Paris Conservatoire was established by the Revolutionary government, to include a national music library containing music and instruments confiscated from deposed nobility and clergy. The law relating to its founding specified that "This library is to be public and open at times fixed by the Institut National des Sciences et Arts, who will appoint the librarian."[6]

In 1964, the valuable holdings of this library were transferred to the Bibliothèque nationale de France, primarily for reasons of preservation. Almost two decades later, in 1814, the Gesellschaft der Musikfreunde (Society of Friends of Music) was established in Vienna, and one of its six formal objectives stated: "The Society will found a music library, which subsequently will be open for public use."[7] The rich holdings of this library today include materials acquired from the Beethoven estate and autograph manuscripts of Schubert, Brahms, and other musical luminaries. And in England, in 1824, music publisher Vincent Novello wrote to a member of parliament, who was also a trustee of the British Museum, expressing concern about the state of the music collections there and proposing that a music department be established.[8] However, no action was taken until 1841, when the flood of printed sheet music from copyright deposits prompted the establishment of a special music section (subsequently known as the Music Room) in the Department of Printed Books, and the hiring of a music cataloger.[9]

Prior to the founding of these early public libraries, there were commercial music lending libraries operated by music publishers and shops in many cities of Europe and the United States. These establishments, which flourished from the eighteenth century through the second half of the twentieth, made music available on short-term loan to largely middle-class subscribers who could afford the modest membership fees, if not the cost to purchase music outright.

## THE UNITED STATES

Americans—preoccupied with a civil war and taming the West—were slow to follow Europe with public music collections. Although the Philadelphia Library Company, established by Benjamin Franklin in 1731, lent music to its paying subscribers, music did not gain much recognition from library administrators until the end of the nineteenth century.[10] Thomas Jefferson's library—sold to the nation in 1815 to re-establish the Congressional library burned by the invading British army a year earlier—included a number of music histories and instruction books, but the former president chose to hang on to his substantial collection of music for performance (he was a competent violinist).[11] The gift in 1894 to the Boston Public Library of the Allen A. Brown Collection of music served as the basis for the first public music collection in the United States. Three years later, in 1897, Walter Whittlesey became the first American "music librarian" when he was appointed chief of the newly established Music Division of the Library of Congress (Boston Public Library did not appoint a music specialist to oversee the Brown Collection until 1907). The Library of Congress music collection at that time consisted almost exclusively of copyright deposits, mostly popular sheet music. Literature *about* music was available in the main reading room. Whittlesey was succeeded as chief in 1902 by Oscar Sonneck, who promptly set about creating the Library of Congress "M" classification for music and music literature, published in 1904.[12]

In 1904, Hiram Sibley donated a 2,000-volume music collection to the library of the University of Rochester in Rochester, New York. In 1921, this collection became the core of the Sibley Music Library of the university's Eastman School of Music, newly endowed by and named for Kodak tycoon George Eastman. Probably the same year as the Sibley donation, Edward Silsky became first chief of the Music Division of the consolidated New York Public Library, although the collection did not open to the public until 1911. Silsky was replaced at New York Public by Otto Kinkeldey, who left in 1930 to occupy the first chair in musicology in the United States, at Cornell University.

Though music for performance was late to appear in American libraries, American librarians were quick to take notice when it did. In 1909, ALA published Louisa M. Hooper's *Selected List of Music and Books about Music for Public Libraries*, intended as a guide to "how best to start a music collection in a public circulating library" (p. 5). This was followed in August 1915 by *Library Journal*'s "Symposium on Music in Libraries," which contained descriptions of music collections and services in the Library of Congress; the Chicago, Boston, and New York public libraries; and in twelve smaller public libraries.

In addition to their collections of printed music, various libraries described in the symposium their soundproof audition and listening rooms, in-house gramophone concerts, and circulating collections of piano rolls. The Forbes Library of Northampton, Massachusetts, reported having a separate music department as early as 1902, when the library was headed by Charles Ammi Cutter, inventor of the Expanded Classification System. The symposium also included information from Otto Kinkeldey about the print catalogs of music held by the Library of Congress and Boston Public Library, a guide to "Music Selection for Public Libraries" by

R. R. Bowker, and an unsigned article on "Embossed Music for the Blind." Something of a breakthrough occurred in 1927, when a subcommittee of ALA's Committee on Cataloging published *The Care and Treatment of Music in a Library*, the first American guide to a broad array of issues about music in libraries.

Whereas the 1915 *Library Journal* symposium surveyed only public libraries, a subsequent survey, prepared by Oscar Sonneck for the Music Teachers' National Association and sent to 2,849 libraries in 1917–18, included academic libraries as well.[13] It reported "the condition and resources of the music sections of public and school libraries, containing 5,000 volumes or over, throughout the United States" (p. 5). Results, presented state-by-state, focused on the number of volumes available and the amount of money spent on acquisitions, and an index referred also to some "special features" reported by several libraries. Of approximately 1,000 libraries responding, 80 indicated holdings of more than 2,000 musical items. Although the holdings and finances of some individual libraries were reported in narrative format, and a few states merited summaries in chart form, details were few. The tone of the report was upbeat, but clearer minds concluded that "exceedingly few libraries are equipped for music research work even of an elementary, non-antiquarian, contemporary kind."[14]

Yet another survey, conducted by Oliver Strunk in 1929 (though not published until 1932),was sent *only* to academic libraries: *The State & Resources of Musicology in the United States*, which included a report on "Musicological Equipment of Libraries."[15] Strunk described the "surprising strength" of the collections in many of the 63 responding academic libraries.

By the 1930s, librarians recognized they were ill-equipped to manage their growing collections of scores and recordings: Techniques to select, acquire, catalog, classify, process, shelve, and circulate them differed from those for books and journals, and there was little to guide librarians in this work. The only professional organizations available to music librarians prior to 1931 were the Special Libraries Association (SLA), which offered them nothing, and ALA, which had made the few tentative attempts described earlier to address music needs. But this was judged by librarians dealing with music to be too little. Consequently, on 22 June 1931, at an ALA meeting in New Haven, Connecticut, nineteen people—eight representing public libraries, eight representing academic libraries and music schools, two representing special music collections, and a private collector—met at the Yale School of Music, elected officers, and created the Music Library Association.[16] Among the topics of concern for this group were standardization of music cataloging, indexing of music periodicals, analysis of the contents of monumental sets of music (*Denkmäler*), cooperative acquisitions, and aids for dating musical editions.[17] Three years after its founding, the association launched its journal *Notes*. George Sherman Dickinson, music librarian at Vassar College, 1927–53, felt compelled to write in *Notes* in 1938 as justification of MLA's existence:

> There is no branch of the library in which there is more placid ignorance on the part of librarians than in music. There is no subject in which there are more complicated problems and more unsolved problems. At the same time, there is no field in which there is more hearty disagreement among those who are supposed to know the answers. . . . Compared with the cases of most alphabetical aggregations, the MLA possesses the supreme reason of reasons for existing.[18]

The Music Library Association has grown steadily since those early years, and in 2008 counted some 1,650 members and subscribers. The annual conference attracts hundreds of attendees, and the quarterly journal *Notes* is well respected for its mix of musicological and practical articles and special features. The association has eleven regional chapters that host their own conferences, and some have publishing programs and exchanges among their members.

# Music Study and Scholarship

## EUROPEAN ANTECEDENTS

Music has been a subject of formal study since ancient times, when Pythagoras (BCE 6th century) discovered the mathematical basis of musical sounds and taught that one who understood musical proportions could also understand the harmony of humankind and the heavens ("the music of the spheres").[19] Pythagorean musical doctrine was transmitted to the Western world of the Middle Ages by Latin writers such as Saint Augustine (CE 354–430), whose treatise *De musica* reviewed Greek musical theory and practice and integrated them with Christian doctrine. Boethius (ca. 480–524), whose *De institutione musica* was one of the most influential treatises of the Middle Ages and Renaissance, and which was still being studied at Oxbridge in the nineteenth century, did not consider a "musician" to be a performer, but one who speculated about music.

From the time of Emperor Constantine the Great and the Edict of Milan (CE 313), which legalized Christianity in the Roman Empire, the Christian church assumed control of education, and *scholae cantorum* (singing schools) were founded to train singers and composers for the church. Music was an integral part of worship, and instruction included singing, playing instruments, and basic elements of harmony and counterpoint. Some musical training was also offered for secular purposes, such as for the town musicians who accompanied civic celebrations. These singing schools were one of the few avenues available for boys to be educated.

With the increase of trade, and the consolidation of secular authority in the nobility, cities grew in wealth and power. Previously, artisans and tradesmen learned their métier through some form of apprenticeship and had little need for the "three Rs." But the new merchant class recognized the necessity of preparation for mercantile and manufacturing occupations and encouraged the founding of municipal schools to offer a broader education than was given in the church schools. Clergy did the teaching, and the curriculum was still largely religious, even though the cities sponsored and controlled the schools. Competition from these municipal schools, along with the upheavals of the Reformation, eventually killed off the cathedral schools.

Until the ninth century, there was no formal system for writing music accurately, so instruction was by oral transmission. Around the time of the rule of Charlemagne (768–814), efforts to standardize sacred chant, so that identical music could be sung in churches and monasteries throughout Europe, resulted in development of more precise written musical notation. The existence of this notation brought with it the need for instruction in its use, and for centuries thereafter, practical musical training focused on reading music rather than on rote learning.

In the medieval universities, music was one of the four subjects— together with arithmetic, geometry, and astronomy—that formed the upper level (the *quadrivium*) of the seven liberal arts (grammar, logic, and rhetoric formed the lower group, the *trivium*). The academic study of music was speculative and metaphysical (*musica speculativa*); it was not related to the study of the art of performance (*musica practica*). Although practical music did not have the same academic respect as *musica speculativa*, the universities provided an environment in which practical musical creation and performance flourished. Music was used extensively for ceremonial purposes, and cathedral and court musicians were typically also university officials. Music's status as a topic of formal study was recognized in 1464 by the awarding of the first recorded doctorate in music by Cambridge University.

In the 1500s, Italian *ospedali* (homes for foundlings, originally attached to hospitals and known in Naples as *conservatorios*) were precursors of modern schools of music. In addition to strong musical training, they usually taught reading and writing and sometimes rhetoric and literature. These schools trained students for the music profession in general, not just for service in the church. The establishment of opera companies in the seventeenth century, and the rise of public concerts in the eighteenth, created a growing need for highly trained musicians, which the early conservatories helped to fill. Many of Italy's greatest composers of the seventeenth and eighteenth centuries taught in the *conservatorios* and *ospedali*, and wrote music to be performed at their profitable public concerts, and many famous opera singers of the day were trained at them.

Outside of Italy, most of the world's great conservatories were established in the nineteenth century. Notable exceptions were the Kungliga Musikhögskolan (Royal College of Music) in Stockholm, established in 1771, and the École Royale de Musique et de Déclamation (now the Conservatoire National Supérieur de Musique et de Danse de Paris), established in 1784 by the Convention Nationale. Not until 1822 was the Royal Academy of Music established in England, organized as a boarding school. A half century later, the Royal College of Music was established by royal charter. These European conservatories continue their musical training missions today.

Modern musical scholarship owes much of its development to German and Austrian scholars, who led the field internationally from the nineteenth century to the mid-twentieth. Johann Nikolaus Forkel, whose *Allgemeine Litteratur der Musik* (1792) was the most comprehensive bibliography of music books to that time, is considered one of the founders of modern musicology, the scholarly study of music; he also wrote the first biography of Bach, *Über J. S. Bachs Leben, Kunst, und Kunstwerke* (1802). Later in the nineteenth century, there appeared for the first time thematic catalogs (*catalogues raisonnés*) of major composers; among the most notable were Ludwig Köchel's of Mozart (1862), and Gustav Nottebohm's of Beethoven (1868). The establishment of the Bach Gesellschaft (Bach Society) in 1850 on the centenary of Sebastian Bach's death initiated the publication of critical collected editions (*Gesamtausgaben*) of works of major composers. The Bach collected edition was followed by collected editions of Handel (begun in 1858), Mozart (1876), Schubert (1883), Beethoven (1884), and others. Similarly, there were government-sponsored projects to publish "monuments" (*Denkmäler*) of early music from German-language areas, the largest being Denkmäler der Tonkunst in Österreich (Monuments of Tonal Art in Austria), begun in 1888, Denkmäler deutscher Tonkunst (Monuments of German Tonal Art, 1889), and Denkmäler der Tonkunst in Bayern (Monuments of Tonal Art in Bavaria, 1900). Around this time also appeared the first journal of serious musical scholarship, the *Vierteljahrsschrift für Musikwissenschaft* (Quarterly for Music Scholarship, published in Leipzig, 1885–94).

## THE UNITED STATES

In the early days of the United States, the church was the primary source of music education, as it had been in Europe. The reportedly deplorable condition of singing in the churches prompted ministers and lay persons to found singing schools in hopes of improving the quality of worship, and the first such school was established in Boston in 1717. Soon, itinerant singing masters were moving from town to town, setting up schools to give several weeks of instruction to locals before moving on to another town. Singing schools inspired the founding of singing societies that set high performance standards, brought outstanding choral works before the public, and provided increased professional opportunities for concert singers and conductors.

After the Civil War, music began to appear in the curricula of public schools. Support came from the growing numbers of private teachers coming out of the singing schools, the increase in choral activities resulting from the growth of the choral societies, interest sparked by the concert tours of international artists, and the impetus provided by the formation of early American symphony orchestras. These developments produced a more musically sophisticated public, which in turn was supportive of music instruction in the schools. Rapid development of music in institutions of higher learning soon followed.

Works of musical scholarship in the United States were rare before 1900. The few music-history textbooks used in conservatories, colleges, and universities were largely translations and compilations from foreign sources. The earliest truly homegrown studies flowed from the pen of Oscar George Sonneck (1873–1928), who was appointed first chief of the Music Division of the Library of Congress in 1902 and served there until 1917. Among his earliest scholarly publications were the dual biography *Francis Hopkinson, the First American Poet-Composer, 1737–1791, and James Lyon, Patriot, Preacher, Psalmodist, 1735–1794*; and *A Bibliography of Early Secular American Music*, both printed for the author in 1905.[20] He conducted his research by studying private music collections and by combing through American newspapers for news of musical events and publications. A decade later, Sonneck lamented that few writers had followed his lead, blaming the lack of opportunities for rigorous training for scholarly research in music and noting that in America, "practically no provision is made anywhere for training professional historians of music as we do historians of other factors of civilization and culture. There has been no demand for them."[21] Although Sonneck was born in the United States, his musical and musicological training was in Germany.

The discipline of musicology finally began to put down roots in American institutions of higher learning between the World Wars I and II. In

1915, the *Musical Quarterly* (the founder and first editor was Sonneck) began, and it continues today as one of the most widely circulated American journals containing serious writing about music. In 1930, the first academic chair in musicology in America, held by Otto Kinkeldey, was established at Cornell University, where two years later the first American PhD in musicology was awarded (Kinkeldey's musicological training also was in Germany). The Nazi regime forced a number of important musical scholars to America's shores, where they taught at major institutions, training the postwar generation of American musical scholars who incorporated their mentors' European methods into the discipline of musicology.

The Music Library Association (MLA) was established in 1931; soon thereafter, in 1934, the association founded its journal *Notes*. Also in 1934, a group of nine music scholars founded the American Musicological Society (AMS), whose *Journal* (JAMS) has been published regularly since 1950. Most members of the society focused on the Western musical historical traditions, but in 1953 the Society for Ethnomusicology (SEM) came into being as a home for scholars more interested in musical ethnography. SEM publishes its own scholarly journal, *Ethnomusicology*. A third direction for musical scholarship was formally recognized in 1977 by the founding of the Society for Music Theory (SMT), whose semiannual *Music Theory Spectrum* has been appearing since 1979.

Formal musical instruction in post-secondary schools in the United States today takes place in three types of institutions: conservatories, music departments, and comprehensive schools of music. The College Music Society's annual *Directory of Music Faculties in Colleges and Universities, U.S. and Canada* for 2006–7 summarizes the disciplines, curricula, degree programs, and faculty research specialties at 1,800 institutions, including conservatories (907 four-year colleges, 375 with graduate programs; 508 two-year colleges, 12 operating only as graduate schools; and 1 institution with no listed description).[22] Most colleges and universities offer at least elementary courses in music history and theory, along with instrumental and vocal instruction. Most also offer instruction in music education, jazz, popular music, and non-Western musics.

Conservatories did not begin to appear in the United States until the second half of the nineteenth century, the first being the Peabody Conservatory in Baltimore (1857), the Oberlin Conservatory in Ohio (1865), and the Cincinnati Conservatory and Boston's New England Conservatory (both established 1867). These conservatories continue to provide professional-level musical instruction today. Their primary role is to train instrumental and vocal performers and composers, with instruction in music theory and history supporting and informing the performance training. Conservatories typically offer pre-college instruction, and degree programs leading to Bachelor of Music (BM), Master of Music (MM), and Doctor of Musical Arts (DMA) degrees. In addition, there are diploma programs concerned almost exclusively with performance studies, without the academics.

Departments of music typically focus on undergraduate and graduate instruction in musicology and music theory with little or no training for performance or music education, though there are exceptions, and instruction in composition is often added to the mix. Music study in undergraduate and graduate liberal arts programs leads to BA, MA, and PhD degrees. Music departments at Harvard, Yale, and Princeton are among the most prominent in the United States.

Comprehensive schools of music are found at many universities, such as state institutions in Indiana, Illinois, Iowa, and Ohio. These combine the features of conservatories and of music departments, turning out performers as well as scholars and educators, granting degrees from the BA and BM through the DMA, Doctor of Music Education (DME), and PhD.

# *Printed Music*

## MUSIC PRINTING

Music has been printed since the time of Gutenberg.[23] Because such a large number of symbols is required to represent music, the music printing techniques developed more slowly than did those for text. Until about the second quarter of the sixteenth century, multiple impressions were commonly required: one for the staff lines, a second for the notes and stems, and sometimes a third for accompanying text. In the 1520s, the Parisian printer Pierre Attaingnant developed fonts that combined note head, stem, and staff lines on a single piece of type that could be strung together with others to form a musical phrase, and this letterpress system was in common use for the next two centuries.

As music became more ornate and complex, letterpress became less suited for its production. Engraving—in which music is drawn in mirror image on a metal plate with a steel stylus or, later, stamped with punches— became a more practical technique. Ink retained in the plates' indentions after cleaning of the surrounding surfaces was then pressed onto blank sheets of paper. By about 1700, engraving had largely displaced letterpress for music, and it held sway until about 1860. Complementing engraving after about 1850 was lithography (and its later refinement, the "offset" process), in which music written with a greasy substance on a stone or plate repels the water-based acid used to eat away the surface of the surrounding area, leaving a raised surface to carry ink to paper. Engraving is still widely used to prepare camera-ready music copy, which is then used to create photographic plates to print the music by the offset process.

In the last quarter of the twentieth century, the use of computers to print music came into its own. A number of music notation programs of varying degrees of sophistication allow input by mouse and computer keyboard, just as a word processor enables the encoding and printing of text. Some notation programs allow input from a MIDI (Musical Information Digital Interface) music keyboard device, as well as playback via MIDI. Among the most popular packages are Finale® (http://www .finalemusic.com/) and Sibelius™ (http://www.sibelius.com/), both available for Microsoft and Macintosh platforms. In addition to their use by major music publishers, music notation programs allow composers and arrangers to self-publish their works with little more investment than the time needed to key in the notes and related text and the cost of paper.

## MUSIC PUBLISHING

The functions of a music publisher include discovering new composers and works and contracting for the rights to produce and distribute them; financing their preparation and printing; promoting them to distributors and to the public; and managing copyrights by negotiating and licensing rights for performance and recording. Many American publishers maintain reciprocal agreements with European publishers to act as agent and distributor for their publications within their respective regions. Publishers of printed music are sometimes categorized as "concert" music publishers (publishers of "serious" music associated with orchestra, opera, ballet, chamber ensemble, instrumental and vocal soloists, and church music); "educational" music publishers (music used primarily by students from elementary school through college, including editions for bands, choirs, and jazz groups, as well as solo and ensemble repertoire for school competitions); and "specialty" publishers (music limited to a particular type of repertoire, instrument, nationality, or even a single composer).

Music collections in academic and research libraries usually include editions from all three categories. Many of the long-established publishers produce "concert" as well as "educational" editions, and "specialty" publishers may bring out editions that fall into both the concert and educational categories. Some concert music publishers undertake critical editions of multivolume historical sets and composers' collected works that feature rigorous editorial practices, as described in the following section. These publications are sometimes  subsidized by foundation or government grants and may take many years to complete.

Although publishing has long been popularly associated with printing, many of today's publishers, particularly of popular music, have no tangible products to sell at all. Instead, they manage copyrights, and collect fees from recording royalties, performances, and radio play. Few pop songs are available to buy in other than recorded formats, the occasional print anthologies of movie and show tunes, and celebrity "folios" of the best-known recording stars. Long gone are the days of mass publication of sheet music of the latest recorded and radio hits, purchased to play and sing at the parlor piano.

## Types of Editions

Selection of music for libraries requires familiarity with the variety of print formats for music and their intended uses. If the score (and parts) are to be used in performance, is the size and clarity of the typeface good enough to be read from a music stand?[24] Will it be used for study purposes only, where a miniature or "pocket" score will suffice? Will it be used by a rehearsal pianist who requires that the original accompanying instrumentation be condensed for performance by two hands on a keyboard? Will it be used for reference purposes, and therefore incorporate rigorous scholarship, historical background information, and description of the editorial precepts followed? The variables are many, as are their possible permutations.

James Grier, in Grove Music Online, identifies four general types of print editions, based on broad editorial and formatting principles: (1) a photographic facsimile of a manuscript or an early edition; (2) a typeset, printed replication of the original notation; (3) an interpretative or performing edition; and (4) a critical edition.[25]

### FACSIMILES

A significant number of the major works of Western art music have been published as facsimiles of the composers' manuscripts, including many composed in the twentieth century.[26] Some are published in microform, such as the monumental project by K. G. Saur Verlag to bring out on microfiche the rich manuscript holdings of works by Bach, Telemann, Beethoven, and Mozart in the Staatsbibliothek zu Berlin–Preussischer Kulturbesitz (the newer section of the Berlin State Library). When complete, Saur's edition is expected to fill more than 6,000 fiches. Similar projects have reproduced the early-music holdings of other great libraries, such as *Music Manuscripts from the Great English Collections*, available complete (994 reels) or in parts from Primary Source Media (http://www.galegroup

.com/psm/); this set includes manuscripts from the British Library, the Bodleian, the Royal College and Royal Academy libraries, and others. Some of the works from the Berlin and English collections have also been published individually in paper format, a few of them in full color with lavish bindings and extensive commentary.[27]

Facsimiles are indispensable to an editor who is preparing a new edition of a work but lacks access to the original sources, and to enlightened performers and scholars wanting to study nuances of notation and phrasing that may not always find their way into edited publications. They cannot normally, however, be used for performance; the original sources may be faded and the handwriting partly illegible; and, in the case of early music, the method of notation unfamiliar except to specialists.

Increasingly, libraries are scanning their early-music sources, including manuscripts, and making them available on the Internet free of charge. These steps provide access to the high-quality images for scholars as well as the general public, while restricting direct access to the originals, which often are fragile. An example is the Pierpont Morgan Library in New York City, which at this writing has begun digitizing its entire collection of more than a thousand music manuscripts, including works in the hands of Bach, Handel, Mozart, Beethoven, Brahms, Chopin, and Liszt, as well as important twentieth-century composers. "The Morgan will also be working with other institutions that house significant music manuscript collections, including the Juilliard School, Harvard University, and the Library of Congress, to develop a unified portal for digitized versions of their music manuscripts."[28]

Similarly, the Sibley Music Library at the Eastman School of Music, Rochester, New York, has digitized many items from its rich collection of early book and score editions and continues to add to this image collection. Scholars and musicians can search or browse this archive at https://urresearch.rochester.edu/handle/1802/292 and download the images for personal use. Visitors to the library's Web site can also request, at http://www.esm.rochester.edu/sibley/?page=request, the digitization of the library's public-domain editions that do not already have images available.

Many modern works are also published as facsimiles of the composers' manuscripts, sometimes because they employ graphic notation systems that cannot be reproduced by standard music fonts and software, and sometimes because facsimiles are simply the most economical way to get the music to the performers. Many works by avant-garde composer

John Cage were published as facsimiles by Edition Peters in the 1960s. Before the introduction of music notation software, this was the format of choice for composers who published their own works, and it is used by many still today.

## QUASI-FACSIMILES

Similar to facsimiles are editions that replicate the original early notation, but use print fonts rather than photographs—quasi-facsimiles. Such editions are used almost exclusively for music written before 1600. The editor can enhance the legibility of the original and make corrections and revisions resulting from scholarly investigation of the work and its sources. The quasi-facsimile is therefore is a type of critical edition (see below). Many scholars and performers prefer this publication format, because they believe that transcription of mensural notation—used ca. 1250 to ca. 1600 to denote metrical relationships between note values—into modern notation, and the imposition of bar lines—which were not a feature of musical notation until the seventeenth century—subtly hinder the performers' interpretations of the rhythmic and metrical flow of the original polyphonic voices. Music originally written in tablature—notation using letters, numerals, or diagrams to specify pitch and duration—also benefits from this type of publication, since details of fingering and voicing can be communicated more directly than in modern notation.

Publishers seem to appreciate that early notations will alienate many potential users of these editions, and some of them compromise by printing the music in parallel modern and early notation, which can increase publication costs substantially.[29] Although such editions usually contain instructions on how to interpret the early notation, the presence of a modern version may discourage novices from making the effort to learn to use the older one, thus partly defeating the editor's purpose. Quasi-facsimile editions are not common.

## PERFORMING EDITIONS

Interpretative editions—also known as practical or performing editions—incorporate aspects of the musical styles advocated by their editors, who are often well-known teachers or performers. An editor may make relatively minor additions to the original sources—a few tempo and dynamic markings, fingerings, phrasings, and the like—while more interventionist editors may actually rewrite sections to suit their own taste. Thus, while such editions may be useful as repositories of information about editors' performing traditions, they cannot be counted on to transmit precisely what the composers wrote. Heavily annotated editions of Chopin's piano music by the French conductor and pianist Alfred Cortot (1877–1962), published in Paris by Salabert, are striking examples of this kind of publication.

By the late nineteenth century and continuing into the twentieth, musical scholars were condemning these practices, and there began to appear editions from which all editorial interventions were expunged, leaving only the notes and performance indications found in the original sources. These came to be called *Urtext* (original text) editions. Today, the term is still widely used but has fallen into disrepute, as it has come to denote not the composer's own written text, but the editor's interpretation of it—that is, ersatz critical editions.

Editorial abuses are now considerably fewer than in the past—though not gone for good—as more performers learn their art and craft in academic settings, where there tends to be emphasis on the original sources for interpretation of the works they perform. The market for performing editions is much larger than for other types of editions, inducing editors and publishers to produce them in quantity, and they vary greatly in merit. Much of the repertory published in these editions has already appeared in scholarly critical editions, and it is to be hoped that a growing number of editors will turn to these critical editions to serve as bases for their own performing editions.

## CRITICAL EDITIONS

The *Harvard Dictionary of Music* distinguishes three types of critical editions: (1) the complete works of a composer—the German term *Gesamtausgaben* (complete editions) is often used by English-speaking musicians to refer to these; (2) historical sets that preserve a musical heritage or repertory—the German *Denkmäler* (monuments) is commonly used by English-speaking musicians—and (3) performing editions published in series.[30] Editions in category (1) are commonly assigned to Library of Congress classification M3 (Collections: Collected works of individual composers), and editions in categories (2) and (3) to classification M2 (Collections: Musical sources). Many libraries treat these editions as non-circulating reference materials or restrict borrowing by other means.

Although editorial standards and practices have evolved since the publication, beginning in the mid-nineteenth century, of the first critical edition of a composer's complete works (J. S. Bach's *Werke*, 1851–1926), a general work-plan for editing critical editions is widely agreed on today. The editor gathers all sources for the work to be edited—composer's manuscripts, editions published during the composer's lifetime, copies or editions with manuscript revisions by the composer, and other relevant documents—collates the sources in a critical report that lists and describes variants among them; transcribes the music into modern notation, making necessary revisions and additions to represent the composer's intentions; and identifies clearly in the transcription and/or the critical report if and how the edition varies from the sources (it is considered a major transgression for the editor *not* to distinguish between what is the composer's original, and what are the editor's interpretations). The critical report should explain the editor's particular choices, and, if the report is extensive, it may be printed in a separate volume. Introductory essays commonly establish the music's historical context, describe the sources, and the editorial methods used. Because critical editing involves many choices, two editors may look at the same sources and come to different conclusions. Critical editions of the same music by different editors, therefore, may look very different on the printed page.

It is now common for publishers to issue selections from their critical editions in formats that are performer-friendly, with the critical reports suppressed, introductory remarks condensed or removed, and piano reductions and/or instrumental parts provided to facilitate rehearsal and performance—stealth critical editions, as it were. Henle Verlag and Bärenreiter Verlag, for example, have published such practical editions extracted from their collected editions of, respectively, Beethoven and Mozart, and A-R Editions has brought out performance versions of selections from its several Recent Researches series.

There are clear advantages to establishing standing orders for the multivolume critical editions that the library is acquiring. Not only is there some level of guarantee that a new volume will not be overlooked, but for many of these sets and series there are significant cost savings for subscribers—and penalties for early cancellation. The standard bibliography of these editions is the 1997 *Collected Editions, Historical Series & Sets & Monuments of Music: A Bibliography*, by George R. Hill and Norris L. Stephens[31], which is a revision of the third edition of Anna Harriet

Heyer's *Historical Sets, Collected Editions, and Monuments of Music: A Guide to Their Contents.*[32] The 1997 revision is an essential guide to the contents of the principal anthologies of music characterized in its title. Since 2004 the data—updated to include collections published since the 1997 edition of the bibliography—have been available also online as Index to Printed Music, Collections & Series.[33] In addition to a bibliography database from the original print publication (ca. 9,300 citations), there is a linked index database (ca. 135,000 records) and name-authority database (ca. 20,000 entries).

Covering some of the same territory as the Hill-Stephens bibliography are the handy guides to "Composers' Collected Editions from Europe," "Monuments of Music from Europe," and "Music Facsimiles in Series," maintained by the German vendor Otto Harrassowitz at its Web site, http://www.harrassowitz.de/music_services/Music_Catalogs.html. Access to these lists is by username and password, available from Harrassowitz on request, and only editions published in Europe are included. For each set listed, the site gives the titles of the individual volumes, their prices (subscription price and non-subscription price), notation of out-of-print volumes, and, in many cases, titles of volumes known to be forthcoming. These listings are useful for determining the availability of volumes when a gap in the numbering is identified in the set on a library's shelves; such gaps often turn out to be volumes not yet published.

## Rental Music

Many concert music publishers reserve some of their copyrighted works for the rental market, making them unavailable for purchase in print. Reasons for this are varied, but, depending upon the particular case, may be to restrict performances to artists and venues approved by composer and publisher, and to limit printing and promotional costs for the few copies needed to satisfy the rental market.

Rental works are usually identified as such in publishers' catalogs, and scores deposited at the Library of Congress for copyright purposes will often be described in a note in the catalog record as "rental material." In bibliographies and composers' works lists, however, they may masquerade as though available for purchase, and if selected and ordered from the library's usual music vendors, the orders will be returned marked "rental only." It is common for library users to unwittingly request purchase of rental-only repertoire for addition to the collection; the music selector who recognizes the telltale rental clues—limited or no appearance in OCLC WorldCat, for example—can save the trouble of initiating a purchase order, and return promptly to the requestor with the news that other avenues must be pursued if a performance is planned. Publishers themselves sometimes are willing to sell scores (but not performance parts) for at least part of their rental catalogs directly to libraries, and a query sent to a publisher's rental department may get a favorable reply about availability for purchase.

Unlike databases and other resources that libraries can lease and access on an annual basis, rental music is intended solely for performers, with terms negotiated on a case-by-case basis depending upon the venue, number of performances planned, admission charge, and other variables. Publishers' Web sites often provide specifics; for example, following the "Rent" link on G. Schirmer's home page (http://www.schirmer.com/) displays U.S. and international contact information, rental instructions and forms, and a link to a downloadable Schirmer rental catalog. Although it is unlikely that a library will become involved in music rental unless it is in the business of acquiring and managing scores and parts for the school's orchestra and choral groups, some knowledge of what to look for in selection sources, and where to direct potential performer-renters, will be of benefit.

## Representative Publishers

The print publishers named below are among the most prominent and influential active in music publishing. Some have been in continuous operation since the eighteenth century, though not always with the same names they now bear. Several are global operations, with offices and distribution in multiple countries. Histories, catalogs, and descriptions of publishing programs are available for most at their Web sites. All—except for one of the youngest, A-R Editions—have entries with additional information in Grove Music Online (http://www.grovemusic.com/).

A-R Editions, Inc., http://www.areditions.com/ (Madison, Wisc., 1962–). Self-described as "the leading U.S. publisher of modern editions of early music," A-R is best known for its seven Recent Researches in Music series devoted to particular eras and genres: Recent Researches in the Music of the Middle Ages and Early Renaissance, Music of the Renaissance, Music of the Baroque Era, Music of the Classical Era,

Music of the 19th and Early 20th Centuries, American Music, and Oral Traditions in Music. New editions in these series are numerous, are widely—and, invariably, favorably—reviewed, and should receive close attention from all libraries with serious collecting objectives. A unique feature of A-R Editions is its copyright-sharing policy, which grants those who subscribe to a series directly from A-R a limited permission to reproduce for study or performance any part of an edition in that series. This license applies to individual subscribers and to subscribing libraries and their patrons, but does not apply to subscriptions placed through other agents.

Bärenreiter Verlag, http://www.baerenreiter.com/ (Kassel, 1924–). Self described as "one of the largest publishers of classical music worldwide," including scholarly collected editions of Johann Walter, Telemann, Gluck, Bach, Gade, Lechner, Handel, Mozart, Rhau, Berlioz, Berwald, Lassus, Schein, Schubert, Schütz and Janáček, as well as of practical performance editions extracted from them. Bärenreiter also publishes important scholarly series of musical editions, including volumes in Das Erbe deutscher Musik (Heritage of German Music, a cooperative endeavor of several publishers), Schweizerische Musikdenkmäler, and Monumenta Monodica Medii Aevi, plus scholarly monographs, yearbooks, congress reports, treatises on instrumental technique and manufacture, and works by contemporary composers.

Boosey & Hawkes, http://www.boosey.com (London, 1792–). In the nineteenth century, Boosey was the English publisher of operas of Bellini, Donizetti, and Verdi. Today, it describes itself as "the largest specialist classical music publishing company in the world"; it controls rights to works of some of the most distinguished composers of the twentieth century, including Stravinsky, Bartók, Copland, Britten, Prokofiev, Richard Strauss, Kodály, Rachmaninoff, Rorem, and Steve Reich. Boosey's principal offices are in London, New York, and Berlin.

Breitkopf & Härtel, http://www.breitkof.com (Leipzig, 1719–). Eighteenth-century publications by Breitkopf included works of Telemann, Marpurg, Mattheson, Leopold Mozart, Haydn, Carl Stamitz, and C. P. E. Bach. In the early nineteenth century appeared Breitkopf's editions of the "Oeuvres complettes" of Mozart, Haydn, Clementi, Dussek, and Cramer—antecedents of the later complete *critical* editions published by Breitkopf—and first editions of a number of Beethoven's works. Between 1850 and 1912, Breitkopf began more than twenty complete critical editions, including those of Mendelssohn, Mozart, Schumann, Schubert, Schütz, Berlioz, Schein, Liszt, Haydn, and Wagner, as well as Bach and Beethoven. The firm was destroyed in a bombing raid of December 1943, but rebuilding began in 1945 with independent operations in Leipzig (East Germany) and Wiesbaden (West Germany); integration in Wiesbaden occurred in 1991 after German reunification. Today, Breitkopf publishes the collected critical editions of Eisler, Hassler, Lasso, Mendelssohn, Reger, and Sibelius, as well as practical editions of numerous contemporary composers and of the classics. Monumental series published by Breitkopf are Denkmäler deutscher Tonkunst, Denkmäler der Tonkunst in Bayern, and volumes in Das Erbe deutscher Musik (a cooperative endeavor of several publishers).

**Broude Brothers,** http://www.broude.us/ (New York, 1930s–). Broude publishes new collected editions of the works of Buxtehude, Jacquet de La Guerre, Lully, Marais, Marenzio, and Rameau. Its scholarly series include Monuments of Music and Music Literature in Facsimile, Tudor Church Music, Masters and Monuments of the Renaissance, and Music at the Court of Ferrara. Since 1981, financial support for publication of these scholarly editions has come from the Broude Trust for the Publication of Musicological Editions.

**Durand,** http://www.salabert.fr/ (Paris, 1869–). Editions Durand is the publisher of works of Debussy, Ravel, Saint-Saëns, Ibert, Milhaud, Poulenc, Messiaen, and numerous other eminent French composers. A collected edition of Debussy is currently under way. Durand shares a Web site with two other distinguished Parisian publishers, Editions Salabert and Max Eschig.

**Carl Fischer,** http://www.carlfischer.com/ (New York, 1872–). In addition to standard choral and orchestral repertory, school music has been a particular focus of the firm, with leading instrumental performers providing arrangements of classical and contemporary works. Fischer was also the publisher of such band luminaries as John Philip Sousa and Henry Fillmore, and still maintains a large catalog of band music.

**G. Henle Verlag,** http://www.henle.de/ (Munich, 1948– ). This firm was founded by German industrialist and amateur musician Gunter Henle to produce practical editions of the classical and romantic repertoire, relatively free of deliberate editorial additions (Henle describes its editions as *Urtext*, but see the comments regarding this term in the "Performing Editions" section). Henle is publisher of the complete works of Beethoven, Brahms, and Haydn, as well as volumes in Das Erbe deutscher Musik (a cooperative endeavor of several publishers) and other scholarly series. Henle editions are noted for their clear engraving and printing.

Edition Peters, http://www.edition-peters.com/ (Leipzig, 1800–). Peters was launched with collections of string quartets by Haydn and Mozart, as well as the first edition of J. S. Bach's keyboard works (fourteen volumes), to which J. N. Forkel contributed the first-ever biography of Bach. Soon thereafter, the firm acquired Beethoven's First Symphony and Second Piano Concerto. Nineteenth-century publications included first editions of Wagner, Brahms, Bruch, and Moszkowski. In the twentieth century, partners in the firm spun off satellite companies in London and New York, reissuing some of the original Peters editions.

Theodore Presser, http://www.presser.com/ (Philadelphia, 1883–). The firm was founded in Philadelphia by a musical philanthropist who had studied at the New England Conservatory. After Presser's death in 1925, the firm acquired a number of other publishers, including Oliver Ditson (founded in 1783, it gave Presser license to proclaim itself the oldest continuously operating music publisher in America). From its beginnings, Presser published *The Etude Music Magazine*, which was directed to music teachers and students, and which by the time of its demise in 1957 had become probably the most widely distributed and influential music magazine in America. Even today, the heirs of untold numbers of piano teachers are offering to donate stacks of *Etudes* to libraries. Theodore Presser is the agent for a number of other publishers, and distributes by sale and rental an extensive catalog of concert, educational, and light music. Among composers published by Presser are Pulitzer Prize winners Charles Ives, William Schuman, Roger Sessions, Steven Stucky, Richard Wernick, and Ellen Taaffe Zwilich.

Casa Ricordi, http://www.ricordi.com/ (Milan, 1808–). The prolific house of Ricordi (more than 137,000 editions by the 1990s) was established by Giovanni Ricordi following several months spent in Leipzig studying the techniques of Breitkopf & Härtel. Soon, lucrative contracts with opera houses in Milan, Naples, and Venice granted Ricordi exclusive rights to publish works composed for those houses, and the firm eventually became the primary publisher of Verdi and Puccini. The firm was bombed during World War II, but most of its rich archive of about 4,000 music manuscripts (mostly autographs) and correspondence survived and is still in the possession of the firm. In addition to the base in Milan, there are branches bearing the Ricordi name in Argentina, Brazil, Germany, and Mexico.

G. Schirmer, http://www.schirmer.com/ (New York, 1854–). Schirmer publishes opera and orchestral study scores, and instructional materials for all instruments. The Schirmer's Library of Musical Classics editions, introduced in 1892, are recognized worldwide by their distinctive yellow covers. The firm published the first edition of the respected *Bakers Biographical Dictionary of Musicians* in 1900, compiled by Theodore Baker, who was Schirmer's literary editor and translator (the dictionary has been updated regularly). Baker was also involved in founding Schirmer's *Musical Quarterly* in 1915 (this respected scholarly journal continues publication today). In 1964, Schirmer acquired Associated Music, whose catalog included a number of internationally known composers. The editions of both firms are now distributed by Hal Leonard, as are the editions of some forty publishers that Schirmer and Associated represent in the United States.

Schott Music, http://www.schott-music.com/ (Mainz, 1770–). Schott was the original publisher of late works of Beethoven and published the first piano scores of several Mozart operas. Works by popular Italian and French opera composers were a Schott staple in the nineteenth century. Today, Schott publishes several music periodicals, including *Neue Zeitschrift für Musik, Das Orchester,* and *The World of Music* and collected critical editions of Mendelssohn, Hindemith, Schoenberg, and Wagner.

Universal Edition, http://www.universaledition.com/ (Vienna, 1901–). Universal Edition (UE) was founded to offer Austrian editions of the classics to compete with those of the German firms Breitkopf & Härtel and Peters, as well as to promote modern composers. The firm expanded rapidly, thanks to an aggressive program for acquiring other companies and the licensing of editions from other publishers for distribution under the Universal name. After a few years of operation, the firm shifted gears to focus almost exclusively on new music, a focus that continues today. During the Nazi regime, UE shifted operations to London. When the Vienna office reopened after the war, the firm continued operations in both cities, once again establishing itself as the preeminent European publisher of modern music.

Wiener Urtext Edition, http://www.wiener-urtext.com/ (Vienna, 1972–). Schott Music and Universal Edition created this group to publish practical and scholarly Urtext editions of eighteenth- and nineteenth-century music. More recently, it has expanded to publish twentieth-century masters as well.

**REPRINTERS**

Reprinters constitute a subcategory of concert music publishers. They perform the valuable service of making available, at modest cost, reprints of public-domain music no longer available from the original publishers. The following firms are reprinters.

CD Sheet Music, http://www. cdsheetmusic.com/. Classical repertoire for printing from CD-ROM or DVD-ROM.

Classical Vocal Reprints, http://classicalvocalrep.com/. Solo vocal music.

Dover Publications, http://store.doverpublications.com/by-subject-music.html. "Over 100 books on music and over 600 scores—piano, orchestral, opera, chamber music, miniature scores, and more."

Musikproduktion Jürgen Höflich, http://www.musikmph.de/musical_scores/information.html. Principally, orchestral and opera full scores of "unjustly neglected" repertoire of the nineteenth and twentieth centuries, with new scholarly prefaces.

Edwin F. Kalmus, http://www.kalmus-music.com/. Orchestral and operatic music, scores and performance materials.

Masters Music Publications, http://www.masters-music.com/. Vocal and instrumental music from the classical era to the twentieth century.

Recital Publications, http://recitalpublications.com/. Classical vocal music.

Edition Silvertrust, http://www.editionsilvertrust.com/. Chamber music works that are "unjustly forgotten or neglected."

## Directories of Music Publishers

**Indiana University Jacobs School of Music, William & Gayle Cook Music Library,** "Printed-Music Publishers," http://library.music.indiana.edu/music_resources/publ.html. More than 725 links to publishers' Web sites and catalogs.

**International ISMN Agency.** *Music Publishers' International ISMN Directory.* 5th ed. Munich: K. G. Saur; Berlin: International ISMN Agency, 2004. Contains contact information for 17,800 publishers or similar institutions involved in the production of printed music, listed both by country and alphabetically. No longer published.

**Music Publishers' Association of the United States,** "Directory of Music Publishers," http://www.mpa.org/directories/music_publishers/. "A listing of contact information for publishers, both domestic and foreign, and copyright administrating offices. The information provided here is submitted by the membership of the Music Publishers' Association, the National Music Publishers Association and the Church Music Publishers Association."

**Deutscher Musikverleger-Verband (DMV),** "Publishers," http://www.dmv-online.com/. The professional association of music publishers in the Federal Republic of Germany, with links to about 500 member-publishers (approximately 90 percent of music publishers active in Germany).

**Music Publishers Association (MPA),** "MPA Members Search," http://www.mpaonline.org.uk/About/members/index.html. The professional association of music publishers in the United Kingdom. Member directory includes links to Web sites, and searches can be limited by musical genres.

**MusicalAmerica.com,** "Industry Links," http://www.musicalamerica.com/. The free "Open to the Public" area includes a searchable database of about 150 publishers in the United States and Canada.

## Music Publishers' Associations

In the United States, three music publishers' associations facilitate communication among their members and keep them current on relevant legal and legislative actions and technology. The Music Publishers' Association of the United States (MPA) is primarily for concert and educational publishers (http://www.mpa.org/); the National Music Publishers' Association (NMPA) is primarily for popular-music publishers (http://www.nmpa .org/); and the Church Music Publishers Association (CMPA) represents about fifty publishers of Christian music (http://www.cmpamusic.org/). Some music publishers are members of more than one association.

## ANNUAL PRODUCTION

There are no comprehensive sources for statistics on printed-music production, as there are for books. The music trade is diverse, diffuse, and largely focused on particular musical communities and repertoires, and this independence has hindered attempts to bring music publishers together in a cohesive marketplace. For example, publishers in the United States have been reluctant to employ the International Standard Music Number or ISMN (originally implemented as "M" plus 9 digits and undergoing conversion to 13 digits, identical to the EAN-13 number encoded in the bar code, starting in January 2008), which was adopted in 1993 by the International Organization for Standardization (ISO) as a counterpart to the ubiquitous International Standard Book Number (ISBN).[34] The latter is a powerful tool that facilitates the collection of data by the R. R. Bowker Company (the U.S. ISBN agency), for the publication of its *American Book Publishing Record, The Bowker Annual of Library and Book Trade Information, Books in Print* (BIP) and its online BooksInPrint.com database, and related publications and collection-analysis tools. Bowker is also the U.S. ISMN administrator but is affiliated only loosely with the ISMN system, not having a full ISMN membership status.[35] Add to this the fact that printed music is ineligible for the Library of Congress Cataloging in Publication (CIP) program, and what we are left with is poor bibliographic control for printed music published in the United States. Nevertheless, there are a few resources that can give some idea of the annual production of printed music that is of interest to libraries.

Theodore Front Musical Literature (http://www.tfront.com/), one of the major suppliers of printed music to libraries in the United States, added 3,864 new score editions to its database in 2007, mostly from United States and European publishers, but also including some editions from

Latin America, the Antipodes, and other parts of the world. While Front makes no claim to have a complete database of new editions, it is intentionally populated with editions thought to be of interest to academic and public libraries that collect music.

The German library vendor Otto Harrassowitz (http://www.harras sowitz.de/) has many customers in the United States for music scores published primarily in Europe, but also offers editions from the Middle East, the Far East, and Oceania. From these geographical sources, Harrassowitz added 4,695 score editions to its database in 2007; a variant search, filtering by *publication date* of 2007, produced 3,065 hits.

J. W. Pepper (http://www.jwpepper.com/sheet-music/welcome.jsp), whose institutional customers include schools and churches as well as libraries, claims to "examine" more than 17,000 new works each year from 3,000 different publishers in servicing customers who maintain blanket orders for scores. Pepper's database, unlike those of Front and Harrasso-witz, cannot be searched to filter by publication date, or by date of addition to the database.

In 2007, the "Music Received" column in MLA's *Notes* listed 535 new score editions. Unlike the "Books Recently Published" column in the same journal, this column does not represent titles cataloged by the Library of Congress (see the "Books" chapter), but only the titles submitted to the journal by their publishers for potential review. These lists are therefore relatively meaningless as indicators of publication output, though they present editions that their publishers believe will be of interest to many readers of the journal (music librarians). Thus, they can be useful for selecting acquisitions. The mean price of the very selective "Prices" survey published in *Notes* of December 2007 for the preceding year, based on entries in the "Music Received" column for which prices could be determined (only 462 editions tallied for this purpose), was $45.67.

Several countries produce national bibliographies that document the annual publication of printed-music editions in their areas of coverage, based on mandatory copyright deposits. Series M of the *Deutsche Nationalbibliographie*, which lists printed music and books about music produced in German-language areas, included 6,174 such editions in 2003 (the last year that this national bibliography of music was produced in print format; it now is published three times a year on CD-ROM, with monthly HTML and PDF updates available to subscribers at http://www .ddb.de). Printed-music editions numbering 3,037 were published in

France in 2007, according to *Bibliographie nationale française: Musique* (http://bibliographienationale.bnf.fr/Musique/BibNatFraMusique.html). The *British Catalogue of Music: BCM*, the national bibliography of printed music for the UK is less than useful for quantifying publishing output. According to the 2006 cumulative volume, it aims to be "the most complete list of current music *available* (emphasis added) in Great Britain." It includes not only all newly published *British* publications deposited at the Legal Deposit Office at the British Library (as mandated by law), but also new music from other countries that is made available in Britain through a sole agent, or that is acquired by the British Library from foreign publishers who do not have agents in Britain.[36]

The print versions of the German and French national bibliographies recently ceased publication. The demise of the print versions renders them less than attractive for browsing for selection in their electronic formats, but potentially still useful for determined selectors purchasing for large music collections.

## EDITIONS IN PRINT

Although no truly comprehensive online music-in-print source exists as of this writing, several online retailers and other resources are helpful in determining what is available and at what prices. In June 2007, the statistics page of Emusicquest: The Music-in-Print Database Online listed numbers of editions in the following categories: sacred choral (152,586), secular choral (122,346), organ (39,687), classical vocal (71,248), orchestral (126,065), string (78,086), classical guitar (34,585), woodwind (70,577), piano (138,797), band (38,603), brass (31,044), chamber (85,431), and miscellaneous (62,502), for a total of 1,047,558 editions.[37] This database is updated several times per month, though the posted statistics are updated less frequently. It should be noted that editions that have been declared out of print are retained in the database, with notes indicating such. Also, in December 2007, the Web retailer Sheet Music Plus (http://www.sheetmusic plus.com/) claimed to offer "456,000+ sheet music titles . . . the world's largest selection," and Sheet Music Service (http://www.sheetmusicservice .com/) claimed in April 2007 to be "home to nearly 270,000 titles of music for bands, orchestras, choirs, vocalists and instrumentalists" (this number had been removed from the Web site by the end of 2007). See also the databases of three library vendors listed in the following section.

The printed-music vendor Educational Music Service (http://www .emsmusic.com/) leases to its customers an annual CD-ROM of its internal working database of music available from all publishers. Out-of-print editions are retained in the database, and their status is so noted. It is not possible for subscribers to extract statistics from this database. Although once-a-year updates mean that the most recent publications are not included, this is a handy resource for installation on the selector's or reference librarian's workstation (license does not allow networking). For additional information and terms, contact EMS at sales@ emsmusic.com.

Bowker's annual *Books in Print*, and its online version BooksInPrint .com, is an unexpected source of information about availability of printed-music editions. Although the preface to the 2006–7 edition of this source states unambiguously that "sheet music" is excluded, there nevertheless are a great many music editions to be found and verified there.[38] In mid-April 2007, an "advanced" search of BooksInPrint.com for the subject term "music," plus format "book," and status "in print," produced 82,056 hits. A large proportion of these were not books, however, but were . . . printed music! Of the 250 titles displayed by this search (250 is the maximum display result for any search), 153 (61 percent) were music. The search results ranged in musical style from the serious (Francis Poulenc's Sonata for Clarinet and Piano, published by Music Sales Corporation) to the lowbrow (*Hal Leonard Ukulele Method*, Hal Leonard Corporation). Some other well-known music publishers represented among the 250 titles were Alfred Publishing, Associated Music, Cherry Lane, Disney, Doberman-Yppan, Dowani International, Edward B. Marks, First Century, Mel Bay, Praxis, PRB Productions, Ricordi, Schott Japan, and Zen-On.

ISBNs are a requirement for inclusion in *Books in Print*. Although not many music publishers assign ISBNs to their editions, the few that do, and who submit them to BIP, apparently can depend upon their being listed there, despite the exclusion claimed by Bowker. Because of this selective representation of publishers, *Books in Print*, therefore, is only incidentally useful for verifying the availability and price of printed-music editions.

# KEEPING CURRENT WITH SCORES

## Notification and Approval Services

Announcements from vendors are essential for learning about what is newly available for selection. The following vendors are among those that provide regular listings of new releases by e-mail.

**Theodore Front Musical Literature,** http://www.tfront.com/. A "new releases" link takes the visitor to Front's site for listings, by month, of new editions added to its database. Displays can be filtered by type (books, music, CDs, DVDs/videos) and by source (United States, Europe, foreign, or all). On request, Front will also send the lists as monthly e-mail attachments. Front's online database contains new books and scores published worldwide since 1994. In May 2008, some 107,000 score editions were listed there. Front offers a European and/or American music-score approval plan; information is available online at http://www.tfront.com/info/approval_plan.php.

**Otto Harrassowitz,** http://www. harrassowitz.de/. Harrassowitz supplies music scores from Europe, the Middle East, the Far East, and Oceania. Libraries can elect to receive print or electronic notification slips based on a profile they define. Also, registered visitors to the Web site can search and display *all* titles with Library of Congress "M" classifications that were added to the database over a range of calendar dates defined by the user. In early May 2008, 137,848 "available" editions with the LC "M" classsification existed in the database. Harrassowitz offers a music-score approval plan for the editions it supplies; a detailed description of this service can be requested at the Web site.

**J. W. Pepper & Son, Inc.,** http://www.jwpepper.com/sheet-music/welcome .jsp. The self-proclaimed "world's largest sheet music retailer" enables signup for its regular Library New Issues e-Club, listing "all the most recent new issues from publishers all over the world. Each data record features the following information: main entry, full title, editors, instrumentation, publisher and place of publication, copyright date, price, and descriptive notes." These lists can be sorted by composer, title, instrumentation, or publisher. Visitors to the Web site can preview a sample issue before deciding to sign up. Pepper also distributes quarterly print catalogs describing a selection of new issues. The company offers a blanket-order approval plan for North American music scores, and claims to examine over 17,000 new works from more than 3,000 different publishers each year to select new editions to offer its customers. Information about this plan is available online at http://www .jwpepper.com/blanket_order.pdf.

In addition to vendors, many *publishers* also distribute e-mail newsletters to inform subscribers about their new editions, and of news and events related to the composers that they represent. Selectors unconcerned about e-mail overload can sign on for as many of these publisher notifications as they would like. Selectors can investigate publishers' notification services through the listing of more than 725 "Printed-Music Publishers" (with links to their Web sites) maintained by the William & Gayle Cook Music Library of Indiana University at http://library.music.indiana.edu/ music_resources/publ.html.

## Reviews

Reviews play only a small role in the selection of printed music, because so few of them are published. A 1985 article on music selection estimated that no more than 15 percent of printed-music editions were being reviewed at that time.[39] Considering that just 611 such reviews were indexed during 2007 in the International Index of Music Periodicals (compare that with 10,198 reviews of sound recordings indexed the same year), and considering some of the annual production figures already noted, that 15 percent reviewed would be an optimistic estimate today. Furthermore, reviews of printed music usually are not published until long after vendors and publishers notify the selector of new publications. Selectors, therefore, must rely on other factors in making decisions about these publications.

## Selective and Annotated Guides

Many hundreds of bibliographies of music can assist the librarian who wants to evaluate and strengthen particular areas of the collection. Particularly useful for this purpose are the bibliographies of music for instruction and performance that in music collections of even a modest size will fill many shelves of the reference collection in the Library of Congress class ML128 (Bibliography, by topic). Bibliographies have been published for just about every imaginable performance medium, from accordion to zither, with all manner of instrumental and vocal categories in between. They vary considerably in quality. Although many are annotated, most are years to decades old; because few are ever updated, they invariably list out-of-print editions. Still, they are important starting points for retrospective collection-evaluation projects. An annotated bibliography of these bibliographies fills some 40 pages of the 5th edition of the standard guide to music reference books, *Music Reference and Research Materials: An Annotated Bibliography*, by Vincent Duckles and Ida Reed.[40]

The standard guide to printed-music repertoire and editions is the Music Library Association's *A Basic Music Library: Essential Scores and Sound Recordings,* 3rd edition (1997).[41] This buying guide is intended for use by librarians who are responsible for collecting music materials. It lists more than 3,000 scores, with an asterisk system indicating titles suitable for small, midsize, and comprehensive collections. For a particular musical work, multiple editions may be recommended. A significant proportion of these editions are still in print, though the stated prices have most likely been superseded. In any case, the manual remains a useful guide to desirable repertoire up to the mid-1990s for printed-music collections.

# *Recordings*

W hen Thomas Edison recorded the human voice on a tinfoil-covered cylinder in 1877, he created the first link in a chain of events that continues to grow today, as evolving recording technologies bring listeners ever-improving audio quality.[42] The cylinder "phonograph" and the flat-disc "gramophone" competed for customers—the first of the format wars—until the 1920s when the 78 rpm shellac disc eventually won public favor. Along with disc recordings came magnetic-tape recorders, developed in the 1930s and in wide use by the end of the 1940s, when the twelve-inch vinyl LP and the seven-inch 45 rpm single were introduced (the "78" became history soon thereafter). Stereophonic playback entered the market in 1952, and by 1956 most companies were releasing all of their recordings in dual-channel stereo. With the popularity of extended-play disc recordings, music that previously had been heard only in concert halls, churches, theaters, and society drawing rooms for the first time became available not just to professional musicians, talented amateurs, and the ticket-buying public, but to everybody.

The introduction of the digital compact disc (CD) in 1982 took the evolution a stage further, with hour-long playing times, elimination of background noise, and enhanced "presence." Record companies exploited the emergence of the CD to remaster and reissue their existing catalogs on the new format, which consumers eagerly embraced. It also sparked an unexpected consequence: a vast expansion of the recorded repertoire. Innovative record companies began to seek out obscure but deserving works—much of it never recorded before, nor likely even *heard* in more than a century—to be recorded by often little-known, though talented, performers and ensembles. No longer were listeners' choices limited to umpteen recordings of the musical warhorses, performed by the usual suspects. The Hong Kong-based Naxos label led the way, and today it has one of the largest and fastest growing catalogs of unduplicated repertoire available anywhere—at this writing over 5,000 titles available on disc and by subscription streaming service. Never have there been more musical choices on record. Call it the Naxos effect.

In 2003, downloading of individual tracks and albums over the Internet to home and portable listening devices became commercially viable when Apple Computer opened its iTunes Music Store. Subscription services also now stream audio into homes and to library workstations. Music-industry Cassandras predict that these latest developments will soon send compact discs to join their shellac, vinyl, and tape precursors in the landfill. That said, most libraries with mature music collections in fact have audio collections representative of decades of responding to the newest formats, and they attempt to provide playback equipment for all but the most ancient and exotic ones.

Field recording has been a tool of ethnologists' research since the late nineteenth century, and since at least the 1950s, recorded music has also been recognized as a legitimate addition to the classical-music research arsenal. Scholars once brought live performers to the lecture hall to illustrate their talks, or they themselves played excerpts at the piano, sometimes reading from a full score and transposing all the instruments of the orchestra to keys and registers that could be negotiated by ten fingers—a skill once common among well-trained musicians, but now largely lost. With the advent of the long-playing record, professors began to challenge music students with "drop-the-needle" quizzes, in which the phonograph's stylus was lowered at random onto a spinning LP for the students to identify the chance selection's period, style, composer, work, movement, or whatever was on the agenda for the day. (Some of the random thrill of this game has been lost with the compact disc, which comes from the pressing plant pre-indexed.) Today, with the study of early-music performance practices; investigation of performance styles and traditions; video preservation and transmission of the work of choreographers, conductors, and opera directors; and increased interest in the study of improvised and other non-notated music and of works "produced" in the recording studio (jazz, ethnic, folk, rock, underground, and so forth), recordings have become primary and essential tools of music research.

# RECORD LABELS

Today, there are four major record companies that distribute their own recordings, and also manage the distribution of other labels ("label" being, in popular usage, the name or trademark of a publisher of sound recordings). Collectively, these four companies control about 70–80 percent of the world music market, and full listings of labels they distribute can be found at their Web sites.

**Universal Music Group** (http://new.umusic.com/flash.aspx), a subsidiary of the French telecommunications giant Vivendi Universal, controlling about 25 other labels including Mercury, Geffen, Decca, and Motown

**Warner Music Group** (http://www.wmg.com/), whose labels include Atlantic, Elektra, Reprise, Nonesuch, and Rhino

**Sony BMG Music Entertainment** (http://www.sonybmg.com/), formed by the merger of Sony Music Entertainment and Bertelsmann Music Group, with labels including Columbia, Epic, Arista, and RCA; and

*EMI* (http://www.emigroup.com/), home to labels such as Angel, Capitol, and Virgin Classics

In addition, there are thousands of independent and private labels, including those of a number of artists and ensembles that have seized artistic control from their former labels, and now distribute their performances on their own private labels. According to Muze, the provider of entertainment media information (http://www.muze.com/), recordings now spill forth annually from almost 100,000 major, independent, and import labels.

## Label Directories

The following Web sites have links to thousands of independent and private labels and their catalogs:

**Allrecordlabels.com,** http://www.allrecordlabels.com/. A database of over 24,000 record label/netlabel Web sites, indexed by genre, format, and location.

**Dirty Linen,** "Record Company Addresses," http://www.dirtylinen .com/. Labels that issue roots, traditional, folk, and world music.

**International Record Review,** "Directory of Record Company Website Addresses," http://www.recordreview.co.uk/. Links to more than 400 classical labels.

**Wikipedia: The Free Encyclopedia,** "List of Record Labels," http:// en.wikipedia.org/wiki/List_of_record_labels. About 2,300 links.

**World Music Central,** "World Music Labels," http://www.worldmusic central.org/staticpages/index.php/labels. A listing by country of international record companies involved with world music or traditional folk music.

# RECORDINGS IN PRINT

## Online Resources

There is no resource for recordings that does what *Books in Print* does for books. Online music stores, which can be counted on to list for sale all the recordings they believe they can supply to customers, may be the best guides to which recordings currently are in print. In May 2008, Allmusic.com—not a store itself, but a music information guide with internal "buy" links from its descriptions of recordings to multiple stores that have them for sale—listed 1,466,125 albums in all musical genres, including 301,064 classical music compositions (these figures are fluid, as the content of the Allmusic.com database, and of others mentioned here, changes daily). TowerRecords.com listed 859,118 CD recordings available, including 143,872 classified as "classical" and 116,871 DVD music video recordings in all genres. The Web site of CDconnection.com has claimed that 400,000 CDs and DVDs "are just a click away!" The Compact Disc Source (http://www.cdsourceinc.com) has reported more than 300,000 CD and DVD recordings available. Fueling the databases of these and other online stores is Muze (http://www.muze.com), a provider of descriptive information on entertainment media. MuzeMusic, Muse's database, claims coverage of more than 140,000 in-print classical music titles, and 900,000 pop music titles, from a total of nearly 100,000 labels. Muze's nearly 900 clients include Yahoo!, eBay, Best Buy, Amazon, Wal-Mart, and—yes—a few libraries, though the subscription cost is likely beyond all but the most flush of institutions (a selective list of Muze clients on its Web site includes only the Library of Congress and the New York Public Library among a number of well-known marketing giants).

Some specialty stores eschew the shotgun approach, and limit their offerings to particular musical genres, providing more focused views of which recordings are available for purchase. In May 2008, ArkivMusic.com, which distributes only classical recordings, claimed more than 80,000 CD, DVD, SACD (super audio CD), and DVD-Audio titles in its database. The classical area of the H&B Direct database (http://www.hbdirect.com) contained 57,893 CD titles, and 2,433 music DVDs. Ejazzlines.com focuses, not surprisingly, on jazz music, and lists more than 30,000 CDs, and 1,300 DVDs. Similarly, TowerRecords.com, which allows browsing by various musical genres in addition to the classical or "everything" approaches, listed, for example, 10,200 compact discs in the folk category, 43,888 in the Latin category, and 21,538 in the show/movie music category. Whatever a library's collecting emphases, these figures show that there is plenty out there to choose from.

## Print Resources

Several non-U.S. periodical publications purport to list the recordings that are available for purchase through retail outlets in their countries of publication, that is, recordings in print in England, in France, and in Germany. For half a century, such a guide was available to U.S. consumers and librarians: the "Schwann" catalogs, which began publication in 1949 as the monthly *Long Playing Record Catalog* issued by William Schwann, a Boston record store owner. *Schwann* was published over the decades with a variety of titles, formats, and frequencies, and the latest issue was rarely far from the reach of librarians responsible for selecting and acquiring recorded music. It was the recordings bible for the United States. *Schwann* ceased publication in 2001, a victim of the new ease of verifying data on the World Wide Web. In at least three other countries, however, such publications soldier on, and they can be quite useful for verification of recording details and availability, particularly of recordings that have not been formally exported for distribution in the United States.

*Bielefelder Katalog Klassik.* Bielefeld: Bielefelder Verlagsanstalt (1953–).
    Semiannual listing of classical-music recordings distributed in

Germany. Title and publisher vary (2006 imprint is from New Media Verlag, Nuremberg). Main listing is by composer name, with indexes by titles, performers, and label names and numbers. An annual *Bielefelder Katalog Jazz* is also published. The 2006 classical volume listed about 46,000 recordings, some 10 percent of which were new to that edition. Since 2006, a Web version has been available for subscription; updates ("Neuerscheinungen") in PDF format are available for free download at http://www.bielefelder kataloge.de/BKK_neu.htm.

*Diapason: Catalogue classique.* Suresnes: Emap France (2002–). An-nual listing of French recordings. Continues *Diapason: Catalogue général classique* (1980–97; publication was suspended 1998–2001). The 2005–6 edition includes 21,000 recordings. Principal listing is alphabetical by composer, subarranged by musical genres. Collections ("Récitals") are listed separately by album title or by principal performer or conductor. Indexed by performer name. Separate listing of DVDs.

*Muze Classical Catalogue.* London: Muze Europe (2006–). Annual listing of recordings in the UK. Online updates are available to subscribers, and the data are also available online to subscribers of MuzeEurope (http://www.muzeeurope.com/), the sister company of MuzeMu-sic. Produced in association with *Gramophone* magazine. Continues *Gramophone Classical Catalogue* (1954–96) and *R.E.D Classical Catalogue* (1996–2005). Titles vary; R.E.D. is the abbreviation for Retail Entertainment Data. The 2005 edition lists more than 60,000 audio and video recordings. Main listing is by composer, with indexes by title and performer; DVD/video and "concert" indexes (recordings containing works by three or more composers) are arranged by label name and number, with cross-references from the composer index. Complete operas are listed separately. Entries for recordings that have been reviewed in *Gramophone* magazine include the date of the review.

## KEEPING CURRENT WITH RECORDINGS

Library selectors of recorded music may be more interested in tracking what is *new* than in what comprises the available totality. In 2004, well over 100,000 albums were issued worldwide, according to the International Federation of the Phonographic Industry (http://www.ifpi.org). A more useful view—limited to those audio and video recordings most likely to be of interest to libraries—can be found in the new-release announcements of vendors that specialize in sales to libraries. In 2006, Music Library Services Company (http://www.mlscmusic.com/) added 14,035 audio and video releases to its database. This figure included 13,403 compact discs in the categories of classical (6,337), jazz (3,540), movie and show tunes (708), and world music (2,819), plus 631 DVDs in all musical genres.

The database of Compact Disc Source (http://www.cdsourceinc.com/CDLIBWeb/Index.htm) contained 6,183 recordings released in 2007 in the classical category in all formats (audio and video), 3,067 jazz recordings, 3,396 international and world music, and 670 movie and show tunes. Far more selective is the database of Theodore Front Musical Literature, a vendor of printed music and music books as well as of recordings; in 2007, Front added 4,183 new compact discs, and 231 new DVD and video recordings.

## Notification and Approval Services

The following vendors of recordings actively solicit libraries' business through corporate membership in the Music Library Association, advertisements in *Notes*, and exhibits at conferences of MLA and other music associations. They provide helpful announcements of newly issued recordings through e-mail newsletters or snail-mailings. Some of these vendors offer library discounts; others do not.

**AAA Music Hunter Distributing Company,** no online database or Web site. To receive an e-mail newsletter containing information about new issues and special offers, contact AAA at 45 Wall St., Suite 220, New York, NY 10005. Phone: (212) 269-7388; Fax: (212) 269-7478; E-mail: musichunter@rcn.com.

**Allmusic,** http://www.allmusic.com/. Registration at the Web site brings a weekly e-mail "New Release Newsletter," including imbedded links to reviews in the Allmusic.com database. It is also possible to browse new releases on the Web site.

**Arkiv Music,** http://www.ArkivMusic.com/. Weekly e-mail updates are available on new classical releases, reviews, and special sales promotions and site visitors can browse new releases. Database contains "over 80,000 CD, DVD, SACD and DVD Audio titles."

**Compact Disc Source / A-V Source,** http://www.cdsourceinc.comCDLIB Web/index.htm. No new-issue notification service is available, but selectors can browse new issues online by release dates. Offers approval plans, OCLC PromptCat MARC records, online order tracking, and shelf-ready processing. Database contains "More than 300,000 CD & DVD titles, updated daily."

**ejazzlines.com,** http://www.ejazzlines.com/. Monthly newsletter by e-mail or post announces new releases (recent newsletters are archived online). Selective print catalogs are also distributed. Database contains 30,000 jazz CDs and more than 1,300 DVDs, as well as jazz books and scores. Includes track and personnel listings, cover art, and sound samples. Downloadable lists of CD and DVD core-collections are provided for four collecting levels. Approval and standing-order plans are available, and discounted library pricing is offered, along with online ordering by purchase order or purchasing card.

**Gary Thal Music, Inc.** No online database or Web site. For monthly mailed bulletins, each announcing about 350 new releases, contact the firm at P.O. Box 165 Lenox Hill Station, New York, NY 10021. Phone: (212) 473-1514; Fax: (212)288-4126; E-mail: garythalmusic @hotmail.com. Bulletin consists of about two pages of general description of several new issues of note, followed by listing by label name of classical "Selected New Releases of Interest," with separate listings of "Musicals & Soundtrack CDs," "Ethnomusicology & International," and DVDs; items of special interest are in bold face.

**H&B Recordings Direct,** http://www.hbdirect.com/. Vendor of classical, jazz, blues, popular, and world CDs, and DVDs that focus on the performing arts. E-mail newsletter about new releases and special offers is sent to subscribers every 7–10 days. Institutional accounts qualify for ordering online by purchase order, and "may also qualify for certain discounts."

**jazzreview.com,** http://www.jazzreview.com/. Sign up online for monthly e-mail newsletter. Web site has CD, concert, and book reviews, feature articles and interviews, jazz news, columns, a forum, and other resources. A searchable CD-review database has thousands of entries.

**Music Library Service Company,** http://www.mlscmusic.com/. Monthly e-mail newsletter highlights significant new releases, and links to lists in PDF or Microsoft Excel formats of new issues in classical and jazz categories. New DVD and world music releases (by music category) and movie and show music (by label) are posted in PDF format only. Web site features core-collection lists and chart and award winners; it also lists in-print titles from the Music Library Association's *Basic Music Library*, 3rd edition. Purchase orders are accepted by mail or through the online database; standing orders and approval plans are available. OCLC MARC records are available for purchased titles.

**Theodore Front Musical Literature, Inc.** http://www.tfront.com/. Monthly lists of new issues are sent as e-mail file attachments or printed cards, and can be browsed online. Classical, jazz, and world music are presented in single alphabetical lists. Standing orders and approval plans are available.

## Reviews

Multiple recorded performances of a musical work may be available for purchase at any one time; for popular works of standard repertoire there may be dozens of versions in print. The compulsory-licensing provision of the U.S. Copyright Act (section 115, http://www.copyright.gov/title17/92chap1.html#115) permits anyone the right to *re*-record and distribute (without the copyright owner's permission) a copyrighted non-dramatic musical work with new performers and interpretations, with the result that contemporary music is also issued in multiple versions. Furthermore, a particular performance may be re-issued by the original label, or by a completely different one.

All of this recording, re-recording, and re-issuing virtually mandates some dependence on published reviews for selection, unless a more haphazard approach meets the library's collecting needs. And, unlike printed music editions that are *rarely* reviewed, a large number of new recordings are commented on in print. A 1993 survey of classical-recordings reviews revealed that 59 percent were being reviewed at that time.[43] The continuing publication of journals that include large numbers of reviews indicates that coverage of new releases and re-releases of classical recordings is still broad today. In 2007, the online International Index of Music Periodicals took note of 10,198 reviews of musical recordings, or about seven times the 1,391 reviews of music books indexed there that year, and more than sixteen times the 611 scores reviewed.

Several print and online journals devote a considerable portion of their content to listings of new releases, and reviews of them.

**Allmusic,** http://www.allmusic.com/. Formerly All-Music Guide. About 50–75 signed reviews of "significant" new classical releases are added per week. Reviews are posted weekly for direct access, and the four most recent weeks' reviews are also available at any given time; thereafter, it is necessary to search for a particular artist or work. An "Editors' Choice" area features "the best of new releases from the past three months" (about 35 entries per month). This resource covers every recorded musical genre in depth, from avant-garde to world music. Entries include complete track information, credits, and sound clips. Classical recordings are given two 5-star ratings (one rating for sound quality, and one for performance excellence); popular recordings receive a single 5-star rating. For print publications based on this database, see the following paragraphs.

*American Record Guide.* About 500 classical reviews per bimonthly issue. Most reviews appear in the "Guide to Records" section, arranged by composer name. Smaller sections cover "Collections," "From the Archives" (historic reissues), "Videos," and a few book reviews. Most issues have an overview article providing extended retrospective reviews of recordings of a single composer or work, or an area of the repertoire. The Web site (http://www.america recordguide.com/) gives subscription information, availability of back issues, brief biographies of the reviewers, a list of recordings reviewed in the current issue, and for registered individual subscribers, access to the text of the current issue online.

*BBC Music Magazine.* "The World's best-selling classical music magazine" (masthead) contains articles, interviews, music news, and about 150 reviews per month, arranged by musical genre, with a 5-star rating system indicating the reviewer's judgment of performance and of sound (two ratings per recording). Focus is on classical recordings, though there are brief sections on jazz and world music. A "disc of the month," reviewed in the issue and accompanied by interviews with the performers, is mailed with each issue. The Web site (http://www.bbcmusicmagazine.com/) includes tables of contents of back, current, and the forthcoming issues, and a listing of 8–10 of the top reviews in the current and preceding two issues. Free online registration gives access to a searchable database of more than 18,000 CD reviews from the magazine.

**CD HotList: New Releases for Libraries,** http://cdhotlist.btol.com/. A monthly "music recommendation service for librarians, from librarians." The list includes about 40–50 thumbnail reviews per month in the categories of classical, country/folk, jazz, rock/pop, and world/ethnic music. The site is hosted by Baker & Taylor, whose customers can order direct from the online HotList. Availability of new lists is announced on MLA-L, the electronic discussion list of the Music Library Association, with a link in the message to the HotList site.

*Fanfare: The Magazine for Serious Record Collectors.* Articles, interviews, label profiles, music news, and about 340 signed classical CD and DVD reviews bimonthly, plus a jazz column. "Classical Recordings" are presented alphabetically by composer name, followed by reviews of collections, arranged by genre (vocal, choral, early music, and others). Some recordings are reviewed by two different reviewers. The Web site (http://www.fanfaremag.com/) posts the table of contents of the current issue, with full text of selected reviews, subscription and back-issue information, and an archive of articles and reviews available to online subscribers.

*Gramophone.* Articles, profiles, interviews, obituaries, music news, and about 125 signed reviews per month of UK releases, arranged by genre: orchestral, film music, chamber, instrumental, vocal, musical theater, opera, and DVD. There is a monthly list of UK new releases. Codes indicate if the reviewed recordings are reissues or historic. "Editor's Choice" highlights a selection of ten of the month's outstanding new discs, excerpts of which are featured on the free CD mailed with each issue. An "Audio" section features brief reviews of audio equipment and new technology. The North American edition includes a "North America Focus" section containing news, interviews, reviews, and a list of new releases on the west side of the pond. The Web site (http://www.gramophone .co.uk/) includes selected news and features, excerpts from the current issue, information about the Gramophone Awards, current competitions and past results, a directory of record labels and their UK distributors, a searchable international concert schedule, and a forum. There is a link to "Gramofile," a free, full-text database of the more than 30,000 compact-disc reviews published in *Gramophone* since 1983.

*International Record Review: For the Serious Classical Collector.* Articles, profiles, interviews, music news, extensive features on major repertoire, and about 100 classical reviews per month, arranged by musical genre and indexed by composer name. DVD reviews are integrated with CD reviews. Includes a listing by label name of international new releases for the month. The Web site (http://www.recordreview.co.uk/) includes a review index and the new-release listing from the current issue, biographical sketches of the reviewers, a searchable concert calendar for the UK, subscription information, and a label directory with links to record companies' Web sites.

Realistically, a selector with limited time and a modest budget could probably rely solely on *American Record Guide* or *Fanfare,* because one journal reviews pretty much the same recordings as the other, as well as those reviewed in *Gramophone, International Record Review,* and *BBC Music Magazine.* But those resolved to plunge in more deeply will want to scan each new issue of all five journals, even though many recordings will show up repeatedly. Through some apparently recurring planetary alignment, these journals seem to arrive around the same time of the month, making the duplications easy to spot. In addition to reviews, each of the journals contains much news about commissions, premieres, prizes, and music-business goings-on that can inform selection decisions just as reviews do, and the U.S. *vs.* UK origin of each journal gives a variety of focus on these matters.

In addition to the five journals named above, numerous others contain reviews of recordings, among them *Downbeat* and *Cadence* for jazz and blues; *Film Score Magazine* for film music releases; and *Early Music America* for early music. It is a good idea for the music selector to scan *all* new journal issues for reviews, ads, announcements, repertoire lists, bibliographies, discographies, or any other feature that can aid in building a collection.

Journals devoted to a particular instrument—*The Double Reed, The Clarinet,* or *Classical Guitar,* for example—include reviews written more from the point of view of the performer and teacher than of the audiophile or collector. These recordings are sometimes overlooked by the more prominent reviewing media because of their narrow focus. It should be noted that these specialist journals often review releases that are two, three, or more years old, whereas the core journals named earlier review current releases.

Few librarians will have the time or fortitude to actually *read* all of the reviews, and it is sufficient on the first pass to merely *scan* them, looking for key terms and phrases like "first recording," or "historic," or "prize," or "essential." Some journals feature an "editor's choice" or a ratings system to attract attention to particular releases. Or, the journal may include two reviews of a recording by different reviewers, indicating that the editor considered it to be particularly noteworthy. Any of these indicators can prompt closer reading of a review. *Gramophone* has its annual awards, which it characterizes as the Oscars for classical recordings. *BBC Music Magazine* initiated its own awards program in 2006, and of course there are the Grammys.[44]

The nominees for these awards in appropriate categories tend to be automatic selections for many libraries, perhaps as a feature written into an approval-plan profile.

Outside-the-box thinking is sometimes required to interpret these reviews, because important information is sometimes omitted. It is not uncommon for a reviewer to neglect to quote a recording's distinctive title or other important contextual information, either in the review heading or in the review text. For a release of Johann Nepomuk Hummel's sacred music on the Chandos label, a 2006 review did not mention that this was volume 3 in an ongoing set titled *The Hummel Mass Edition*, information that might have led the selector to check further on the holdings or availability of the preceding two releases.

This apparent lack of attention extends also to the labels themselves. A 2005 release titled *The Music of Mario Davidovsky*, volume 3, on the Bridge label, was preceded by issues in 2000 and 2002 of the composer's works, though neither of those bore the *Music of. . .* title or a volume number. In this case, hindsight may have influenced the marketing department: "Eureka! I think we can turn this into a multi-volume set!" In such cases the selector's opportunity to establish a standing order for the set may be hindered. It is not uncommon for such "sets," when complete, to be reissued as a single package.

While title reigns supreme as an identifier for books, it is of secondary importance in many sound-recordings reviews.[45] In other cases, a musical work that *does* have a distinctive title may be quoted only in an

English translation of whatever language is used on the recording itself. In a mid-2007 review, a reviewer for a well-known publication retitled Gian Francesco Malipiero's opera *Giulio Cesare* as *Julius Caesar*—a potential tripping point for indexer, selector, and pre-order searcher alike.

## Popular Music

Although much more popular music is released, the popular genres are reviewed less frequently than classical music; a study in 1989 found that fewer than 12 percent of popular music recordings were then being reviewed.[46] Not much seems to have changed since then; typically, a handful of reviews show up in popular journals aimed at consumers of this music. Among these are *Spin* (http://www.spin.com/), *Rock Sound* (http://www .rock-sound.net/) and *Q: The Essential Music Guide* (http://www.q4music .com/); *Downbeat* (http://www.downbeat.com/) for jazz and blues; and *Dirty Linen* (http://www.dirtylinen.com/) for folk and world music.

In lieu of reviews, collectors of recordings of popular-music genres will find the "charts" printed in *Billboard,* the major music-industry weekly, to be useful. A chart is "a list of songs or records graded in terms of popularity, generally measured in terms of record sales, radio airplay or both."[47] *Billboard* was first introduced in 1894, and in 1935 published its first "hit parade"—a term then used to rank popular songs. Five years later came its first "Music Popularity Chart," and by 1958 the "Hot 100 Chart" was a staple of each issue. Today, *Billboard* publishes some twenty charts for various musical genres; in addition to mainstream pop music, these include rhythm and blues, country music, gospel and contemporary Christian music, New Age, classical, "classical crossover," and additional categories. Each *Billboard* issue also contains around thirty reviews.

*Billboard* is widely held by libraries, both academic and public, and can be found at well-stocked newsstands. Selectors without access to the print or online full-text editions of *Billboard* can find abbreviated versions of the current and preceding week's charts (only the top ten or so sellers in each category) posted at *Billboard*'s Web site (http://www.billboard .com/bbcom/charts/genre_index.jsp) and at the Web site of the recordings vendor Music Library Services Company (http://www.mlscmusic.com/). The data source for these charts is Nielsen SoundScan (http://www.sound scan.com/), an information system that tracks sales of music and music video products throughout the United States and Canada, based on figures

collected weekly from over 14,000 retail, mass merchant, and other outlets (Nielsen, under the banner of Nielsen Media Research, also famously
ranks TV networks, affiliates, and programs).

## Folk and World Music

The following Web sites contain information about new recordings of folk
and world music. They do not have e-mail newsletters, so it is necessary for
the selector to visit the sites to view information about new releases.

**Dirty Linen,** "New Releases," http://www.dirtylinen.com/. Online list of all
new recordings and DVDs as listed in the current issue of the paper
journal. Information is minimal: artist name, album title, and label
name. Reviews are published in the print journal of the same title.

**Ethnomusicology,** "ographies," http://webdb.iu.edu/sem/scripts/publica
tions/ographies/ographies.cfm. Geographical listings of "Current Discographies" and "Current Films and Videos" are given at this Web site of
the journal *Ethnomusicology.* Listings are organized according to volume and issue numbers of the journal, though the lists are published
exclusively online. Recordings are not reviewed here, though the print
journal does include a few reviews.

**WorldMusicStore.com,** http://www.worldmusicstore.com/. The sales out-
let for Multicultural Media. A "New Releases" area provides details of
several hundred recordings; there is no statement about how long a
release is considered "new." The database contains "almost 12,000 titles
of traditional and contemporary world music compact discs, videos
and DVDs."

## SELECTIVE AND ANNOTATED GUIDES

For selectors seeking to build retrospective collections of recordings, several buying guides can aid the selector in filling gaps.

***A Basic Music Library: Essential Scores and Sound Recordings,*** 3rd ed.
Compiled by the Music Library Association; Elizabeth Davis, coordinating editor; Kent Underwood and William E. Anderson, sound
recordings editors. Chicago: ALA, 1997. A buying guide "intended for

use by librarians who are responsible for collecting music materials. . . . its listings are both systematic and selective; and it represents the music world in a way that is balanced and diverse, culturally and geographically" (preface). Lists 7,000 recordings, with an asterisk system indicating recordings suitable for small, midsize, and comprehensive collections. The recording listings "are worldwide in scope, including classical, traditional, and popular musics of the Americas, Europe, Africa, and Asia." The recordings recommended in the current edition are likely to be out of print, though some may have been reissued with different label details. It remains useful as a guide to recommended *repertoire* recorded up to the mid-1990s. A new edition is in preparation.

**Christgau Consumer Guide,** http://www.robertchristgau.com/cg.php. Robert Christgau (the "dean of American rock critics," according to the Web site), former music critic for the *Village Voice*, and at this writing a contributing editor for *Rolling Stone*, by December 2007 had here graded 13,652 rock albums from 5,796 artists on 2,387 labels, with 11,817 reviews.

*The Gramophone Classical Good CD, DVD & Download Guide: 2007.* Teddington, Middlesex, Eng.: Haymarket, 2006. The latest, at this writing, in a series of occasional buying guides from the publisher of *Gramophone* magazine. Title varies. Contains unsigned, paragraph-length reviews by fifty-nine contributors, arranged alphabetically by composer name. Collections (three or more composers) are listed separately in the classifications of orchestral, chamber, instrumental, choral, vocal, and early music, and are indexed by composer/title. There also is an index of artists. Special features include a guide to Internet downloading, a list of "100 Great Recordings," a suggested basic-library repertoire list, and narrative introductions to "Understanding Early Music"; the music of the baroque, classical, and romantic eras; and "new" music. Codes identify general price ranges, historic recordings, use of period instruments, and four levels of musical and recording excellence.

*Penguin Guide to Compact Discs and DVDs Yearbook.* By Ivan March, Edward Greenfield, and Robert Layton. London: Penguin, 2002–. Annual. Published since the 1970s with varying titles. The 2006/07 edition is the most comprehensive survey of classical music on CD and DVD, listing and evaluating about 1,300 recordings. Uses a 4-star rating system, with "rosettes" awarded to particularly worthy recordings. New and reissued recordings included in each edition are so indicated. The *Penguin Guide* has been criticized for its bias in favor of British composers, conductors, ensembles, soloists, and labels, and should therefore be used by American librarians in tandem with other resources.

*Penguin Guide to Jazz Recordings.* By Richard Cook and Brian Morton, 8th ed. London; New York: Penguin Books, 2006. Published biennally since 1992 in revised editions and with varying titles. The 2006 edition reviews 14,000 CDs (including 2,000 new since the previous edition), with a 4-star rating system in addition to the written evaluations. Two hundred recordings named by the authors as suitable for a core collection are identified throughout the book, which is organized by artists' names. Indexed by group and by group members' names. A companion volume is *Penguin Guide to Blues Recordings* by Tony Russell and Chris Smith, also published in 2006.

Two series of print volumes, the All Music Guides and the Rough Guides, can guide the selector of particular musical genres. The All Music Guides (published by Backbeat Books) are print compilations based on the Allmusic.com Internet source described earlier under "Recordings in Print." At this writing, there are printed All Music Guides to classical music (published 2005), country music (2nd ed., 2003), electronica (2001), hip-hop (2003), jazz (4th ed., 2002), rock (3rd ed., 2002), soul (2003), and blues (3rd ed., 2003). These titles are available from book retailers, but not through Allmusic.com.

http://www.roughguides.com/website/reference/music/default.aspx. The Rough Guides print series is described at this Web site and includes volumes devoted to blues (2007), classical (2005), country (2000), heavy metal (2005), hip-hop (2005), jazz (2004), music USA (popular genres, 1999), opera (2002), punk (2006), reggae (2004), rock (2003), soul and R&B (2006), and world music (2 vols., 2000–2006).

## Pricing

Unlike printed music, where editions of fewer than fifty pages can range in price from a few dollars to hundreds, the pricing of sound recordings is relatively consistent. Rarely does a single compact disc cost over twenty dollars, and discs on budget labels can be purchased for little more than five. In some reviewing sources, prices of sound recordings are conveniently categorized in three or four price ranges. For example, in the Gary Thal Music bulletins described under "Notification and Approval Services," releases are classified as "budget" ($5–$9), "midprice" ($10–$14), and "full price" ($14 and up). *BBC Music Magazine* uses a one-to-three £-symbol coding system to represent budget (up to £6.99), midprice (£7–£11.99), and full price (from £12). *Gramophone* magazine uses a four-tier system of superbudget (£5.99 and below), budget (£6–£7.99), midprice (£8–£10.99), and full (£11 and above).

As a rule, prices of recordings are consistently higher in Europe than in the United States, even though a disc categorized as "budget" by a UK journal may graduate to "midprice" or more when imported into the United States. Although these price-ranges are inexact, they can assist in estimating an amount to commit when placing an order if the publisher's recommended list price is not immediately known. In any case, as noted earlier, publishers' list prices are discounted by some library vendors, not by others. Online stores usually state the publisher's price, and the discount price if any is offered.

## Audio Streaming Services

Subscription databases of digitized audio that can be streamed to library users' workstations can increase the repertoire available to listeners, and reduce the library's costs to select, acquire, catalog, and physically process individual recordings. The disadvantage, however, is that the library is buying pigs in a poke; the particular works and performances provided are selected by the service, not by the library.

These audio streaming services incorporate custom playlists and static URLs to address local curriculum needs. Subscription costs are typically based on the number of simultaneous listeners that the subscribing library is able to support. The descriptions that follow are quoted from the services' Web sites as they appeared in December 2007.

African American Song, http://www.alexanderstreet.com/products/ aamu. htm. "*African American Song* brings 50,000 tracks of music to the ears of library patrons and music scholars. It's the first online resource to document the history of African American music in the form of an online listening service. . . . The collection contains recordings by the top names in the history of black American music . . . and at least 5,000 of the tracks are rare or never-before-published. The other 45,000 tracks are in-copyright and licensed from various labels. The entire available catalog of Document Records—the world's largest collection of rare and vintage blues, jazz, gospel, spiritual, boogie-woogie, and country recordings—is included. . . . Through arrangement with Rounder Records, another major independent label specializing in blues, folk, gospel, jazz, reggae, roots, and soul music, *African American Song* will deliver online access to the Alan Lomax Collection . . . an unrivaled assemblage of international field recordings by folklorist Alan Lomax from the 1930s through the 1960s. . . ."

**Classical Music Library,** http://alexanderstreet.com/products/clmu.htm. "*Classical Music Library* is a fully searchable classical music resource— a comprehensive database of distinguished classical recordings. It includes tens of thousands of licensed recordings that users can listen to over the Internet. The audio selections are cross-referenced to a database of supplementary reference information. . . . *Classical Music Library* is the only audio service that is developed exclusively with the needs of librarians in mind. . . . It's . . . built on a musically authoritative database that is structured around works and performances rather than CDs. . . . Content is published under licensing agreements with more than 30 music labels, including major labels and independents, with ongoing license negotiations adding to the range of available tracks. . . . The service works on PCs or Macs and . . . the library can choose whether or not to allow users to download tracks to a portable storage or player device."

**Database of Recorded American Music (DRAM),** http://www.dramonline .org/. "DRAM is a not-for-profit resource providing CD quality audio, complete and original liner notes and essays from New World Records, Composers Recordings, Inc. (CRI) and other important labels. . . . Currently, there are over 1,500 CDs (9,800 compositions) on DRAM . . . from folk to opera, Native American to jazz, 19th century classical to early rock, musical theater, contemporary, electronic and beyond. . . . As of 2007, much of the DRAM collection comes from the New World and Composers Recordings catalogue. Other partners include Albany Records, Artifact Recordings, Cedille Records, Cold Blue Music, Deep Listening, Frog Peak Music, innova Recordings, Mutable Music, Pogus Productions, and XI."

**Naxos Music Library,** http://www.naxosmusiclibrary.com/. "Naxos Music Library (NML) offers not only practically all standard repertoire, but also an enormous range of specialist repertoire not available from other online sources. The recordings in Naxos Music Library include the complete catalogues of BIS, Chandos, CPO, Hänssler, Hungaroton, Marco Polo, Naxos and selected titles of other leading independent labels, with more labels being added from time to time. . . . Naxos Music Library is the most comprehensive collection of classical music available online. It includes . . . over 262,000 tracks, including Classical music, Jazz, World, Folk and Chinese music."

**Naxos Music Library Jazz,** http://www.naxosmusiclibrary.com/jazz/. "Naxos Music Library Jazz is one of the most comprehensive collections of Jazz music available online. It offers close to 22,600* tracks of jazz from over 2,300* albums. Over 500* jazz artists are represented. Naxos Music Library Jazz comprises Naxos Jazz and the 22 labels of Fantasy Jazz. Naxos Jazz, along with Prophone and Proprius, brings you the world of international Jazz, covering Sweden and Scandinavian jazz artists. U.S.-based Fantasy has the world's deepest jazz catalogue and offers the very best in blues and R&B. All these can be accessible from computers in academic libraries, home or office (*As of August 2007)."

**Smithsonian Global Sound,** http://www.alexanderstreet.com/products/glmu.htm. "*Smithsonian Global Sound for Libraries* is a virtual encyclopedia of the world's musical and aural traditions. . . . The database includes an extraordinary array of more than 35,000 individual tracks of music, spoken word, and natural and human-made sounds. . . . Specially developed controlled vocabularies . . . enable users to browse by musical instrument, geographic area, or cultural group, among other fields. . . . *Smithsonian Global Sound for Libraries* includes the published recordings owned by the non-profit Smithsonian Folkways Recordings label and the archival audio collections of the legendary Folkways Records, Cook, Dyer-Bennet, Fast Folk, Monitor, Paredon and other labels. It also includes music recorded around the African continent by Dr. Hugh Tracey for International Library of African Music (ILAM) at Rhodes University as well as material collected by recordists on the South Asian subcontinent from the Archive Research Centre for Ethnomusicology (ARCE), sponsored by the American Institute for Indian Studies."

# *Books*

## ANNUAL PRODUCTION

The number of books about music published in the United States is relatively small, and short print runs of around 500–1,000 copies for scholarly titles are the norm.[48] In 2006, American book production included 744 titles with the primary subject of music, according to the year's cumulative listing in *American Book Publishing Record* (ABPR).[49] Included in that listing were titles with a subject-heading subdivision "Juvenile literature" (11.7 percent of entries), and reprints. About 18 percent of the 744 titles were hagiographies of pop-music stars and groups—an encouraging indication that some fans of this music actually turn the volume down long enough to read about it. Most books of this type will more likely be additions to public-library browsing collections than to academic library collections.

The 2007 *Bowker Annual of Library and Book Trade Information* posted a startlingly larger number than ABPR for music books published in 2006: a "preliminary" tally of 2,145. The discrepancy can be explained by the two publications' different sources of data; in 2000, the *Bowker Annual* began reporting data from *Books in Print* (BIP) rather than from the *American Book Publishing Record*. *Books in Print* recognizes three formats (books, audio, and video), and printed music that carries an ISBN number—not all music publishers use these, but many do—is dumped into BIP's "book" category, thus skewing the numbers (the quantity of printed music in *Books in Print* is described elsewhere). The ABPR listings, on the other hand, are taken from MARC cataloging records created by the Library of Congress for its Cataloging in Publication Program (CIP). Because printed music is excluded from CIP, none finds its way into the ABPR.[50]

Annual book-publishing numbers in some other countries are also of interest, since academic libraries usually collect beyond U.S. borders, and in languages other than English. These countries maintain national bibliographies that document their book-publication output (the United States does not produce a national bibliography). German-language publications on music are recorded in *Deutsche Nationalbibliographie, Reihe M: Musikalien und Musikschriften.* The most recent publication of this national bibliography in print form was in 2003, when it listed 1,811 books on music; the bibliography is now updated for subscribers on CD-ROM, and with monthly HTML and PDF files at http://www.ddb.de/. In France, 335 books on music were published in 2007, according to *Bibliographie nationale française: Livres* (http://bibliographienationale.bnf.fr/Livres/Bib NatFraLivres.html). The *British National Bibliography* for 2006 listed 975 books on music; many of these were British issues of titles also published in the United States.

For librarians, a perhaps more practical measure for music-book production is found in the database of Theodore Front Musical Literature (http://www.tfront.com/), a music, recordings, and music-book vendor to libraries world-wide. In 2007, Front added 830 new books that it believed would be of interest to its clients; these were primarily in English, but there also were some titles in French, German, Italian, and Spanish. Searches in Front's database can be filtered by format, and by the year and month added.

## EDITIONS IN PRINT

### United States

Since 1948, the R. R. Bowker Company (http://www.bowker.com/), with corporate headquarters in New Providence, New Jersey, has been keeping librarians and booksellers informed, with its annual *Books in Print* series and its supplements, of the U.S. books that are available for purchase. Today, Bowker's standard is the online BooksInPrint.com, to which many libraries subscribe. In mid-April 2007, an "advanced" search of that database for books assigned the Library of Congress class "ML" (music literature) and a status of "in print" produced 22,197 hits. Note, however, that a broader search using "music" as a subject word, instead of limiting to LC class ML, produced nearly four times as many hits. The latter search drew in books assigned other LC classifications, or with LC classification omitted from the entry but with sufficient musical content to merit "music" as a subject term. A significant number of printed-music editions also found their way into the database, as well as into the print version of *Books in Print*, despite the stated exclusion in the preface to the print edition, where "sheet music" is one of several named classes of excluded materials. For more information about the anomalous inclusion of printed music in *Books in Print*, see the chapter on "Printed Music."

As readers have come to expect to find just about any in-print book published in the United States found for sale at Amazon.com, Barnes andnoble.com, and other online bookstores, so librarians have discovered the convenience of those sites for verifying availability and prices of books needed for the library. Many entries at these bookstore sites also are accompanied by the texts of reviews from *Publishers Weekly*, *Choice*, and other reviewing sources familiar to librarians, as well as some reviews contributed by customers.

## Abroad

Sources analogous to BooksInPrint.com document the availability of books for sale in other countries. Here are three:

**Verzeichnis lieferbarer Bücher** (Catalog of Available Books) for German-language books, available free for searching at http://www .buchhandel.de/.

**Libros en venta en Hispanoamérica y España** (Books for Sale in Latin America and Spain), formerly available for free access, but now marketed by NISC at http://www.nisc.com/.

**Bowker's GlobalBooksInPrint.com,** for bibliographic coverage of Australia, Canada, U.S., UK, New Zealand, and South Africa.

Online bookstores in other countries can serve the same in-print verification function as Amazon.com and Barnesandnoble.com for U.S. imprints. Amazon.com has, as of this writing, six international outposts: Canada, France, Germany, the UK, plus China and Japan, for collectors in those languages. Links to these non-U.S. stores are on the U.S. Amazon. com Web site.

European library-vendor databases also serve, for practical purposes, as books-in-print resources for the regions and languages they distribute. For Germany and Austria, the database of Wiesbaden-based Otto Harrassowitz (http://www.harrassowitz.de/) adds virtually the same new music-books as are listed in the monthly *Deutsche Nationalbibliographie, Reihe M*, mentioned above. And titles added to OttoEditions seem to remain there for reference purposes even after going out of print, though with appropriate annotations. The situations are similar at the vendor Jean Touzot Librairie Internationale site for French books (http://www.touzot.fr/), and Casalini Libri for Italian books (http://www.casalini.it/). All three of these library vendors—Harrassowitz, Touzot, Casalini—provide specialized service to American libraries, and have Web interfaces in English. Their databases can also be searched with reference to LC classification "ML" (music literature), and filtered by the dates that titles were added to the databases (or by publication dates), so that returning selectors can readily see what music books have been added since the previous visit. These vendors also have notification and approval services, as described in "Keeping Current with Books." Registration is required to access the Casalini and Harrassowitz data; access to Touzot data is unrestricted.

# KEEPING CURRENT WITH BOOKS

## Notification and Approval Services

Many libraries have institutional notification and approval plans established through a U.S. book vendor, and the music selector will likely have access to such a service. These plans may also cover books published in the United Kingdom.

Music selectors might also want to investigate Bowker's BIP Alert Service. Both librarians and patrons at libraries subscribing to BooksInPrint.com can sign up on the library's Web page to access the service, which provides monthly e-mail notifications of new titles that fit saved search criteria. A saved search that includes the LC class "ML" in its criteria will harvest citations for new books about music added in the previous month, and the selector can opt to view new *forthcoming*, or only newly *published* titles. A search that specifies, instead, the *subject word* "music" will retrieve citations included in the "ML" search, plus other books with music content, regardless of their LC classification, and the many editions of printed music that are added to BooksInPrint.com.

Although the Bowker BIP search method is quick and efficient, it has some limitations. Information as submitted by publishers is sometimes incomplete or incorrect—a book that eventually is assigned an ML classification when cataloged by a library may not be so labeled when first added to BooksInPrint.com. Furthermore, a broad search will likely retrieve more hits each month than the system's 250-item display limit.

Non-U.S. library vendors also have approval, and slip or e-mail notification services that can benefit selectors who collect books in languages other than English. Registered users of these vendors can establish profiles to receive notifications in specific subject areas of interest, delivered in the preferred format. Otto Harrassowitz notifies of new books published in Germany, Austria, and Switzerland in all languages. Casalini Libri notifies of new books published in Italy, France, and Spain. Jean Touzot notifies of French-language books published in France, as well as in Belgium, the Netherlands, Switzerland, Africa, Canada, and other francophone regions. Puvill Libros (http://www.puvill.com/) notifies of books published in Spain, Portugal, Mexico, Andorra, and parts of Latin America.

## Print Notifications

The following music periodicals have noteworthy books-received columns. Although books do not appear in the lists until significantly after their actual publication dates, the lists are useful in identifying titles that may have escaped notice by other, more current notification sources.

*Fontes Artis Musicae,* "Recent Publications in Music," compiled and edited annually by Geraldine E. Ostrove of the Library of Congress. *Fontes,* the quarterly journal of the International Association of Music Libraries, Archives, and Documentation Centres (IAML), "contains citations to literature about music in print and other media, emphasizing reference materials and works of research interest. . . ."[51] The most recent installment (Oct.–Dec. 2006) at the time of this writing contained 1,726 entries published mainly the year preceding the list, with some retrospective titles from up to the previous five years, submitted by contributors from 26 countries. Approximately one-third of the entries were from countries whose primary language is English. English translations of titles are provided for other entries. Though listing in *Fontes* often postdates a book's publication by up to two years, and publication of the journal tends to run somewhat behind schedule, there is a high concentration here of citations for research books that go unnoticed elsewhere. It is an essential selection source for music research libraries.

*Music & Letters,* "Books Received" column in each quarterly issue. Publishers submit new scholarly books in hopes of reviews in this respected British musicological journal. About 75 new titles are listed in each issue, with full bibliographic citations.

*Notes,* "Books Recently Published" column in each quarterly issue. "This column is compiled quarterly, based on the output of the monographic music cataloging units of the Library of Congress. Entries appear on the list as they are cataloged by the library, regardless of the date of publication" (headnote of each column). These lists, therefore, can substitute for the music-book entries from the Library of Congress Cataloging Distribution Service's (CDS) "Books All" service, which weekly distributes MARC records to subscribers, including CIP (Cataloging in Publication) records for books and serials recently cataloged by LC.[52] In 2006, the *Notes* columns listed 1,734 books: 843 in English, 264 in German, 46 in Italian, 122 in Spanish, 170 in French, 82 in Russian, and 207 in Albanian, Afrikaans, Azerbaijani and a Babel of 32 other languages. Although these are not annual *publication* figures (they include some titles published earlier, but only now being cataloged by the library), they do represent the numbers and types of books entering one of the world's most comprehensive music collections in a single year.

**Society for Ethnomusicology,** "Current Bibliographies," http://webdb.iu .edu/sem/scripts/publications/ographies/ographies.cfm. A geographical listing by subject of recent print and Web publications in the field of ethnomusicology. Includes articles as well as books. Listings are organized according to volume and issue numbers of the journal *Ethnomusicology,* though the lists are published exclusively online.

## Standing Orders

Many scholarly books about music are published as volumes in numbered series, some in the United States, but many more in Germany and Austria, where there seem to be dozens of musicological monographic series bringing out revised dissertations. Among the publishers of these German-language series are Laaber-Verlag, Peter Lang, and Hans Schneider, all three of which produce several series. Publishers know that demand for these books will be small, even for those in English, and perhaps they hope to guarantee at least a minimal return on their investments by enticing libraries to establish standing orders for their series. This approach seems to work, at least in part, for the publishers that have developed reputations among librarians for producing books of sound scholarship. It also works to the benefit of subscribing libraries by guaranteeing the receipt of the series' current titles.

Several U.S. publishers, identified elsewhere in this publication, are now bringing out important musicological research, and several of them produce monographic series worthy of selection as potential standing orders. At this writing, there is no current and comprehensive bibliography of music monographs in series like that of Hill and Stephens's *Collected Editions, Historical Series & Sets & Monuments of Music* for printed music (see the chapter on printed music).[53]

## REVIEWS

Reviews of scholarly books on music seem to play a relatively insignificant role in their selection. In 2007, the International Index to Music Periodicals (IIMP) indexed 10,198 reviews of musical audio and DVD recordings, compared to only 1,391 reviews of music books. Scholarly books are aimed at academics who must keep up to date in their fields. They are published in short print runs and are not heavily promoted; they make little or no profit for their publishers. Many are published by university presses, which may be subsidized by their host institutions. Libraries need to acquire such books long before reviews appear, which is typically more than a year after the books are published and long past a reasonable sell-by date for faculty and students eager to get their hands on them. For selection purposes, therefore, reviews are useful primarily for titles that were not of great enough interest to purchase at the time of their publication, or that were overlooked by sources that regularly report new releases.

However, reviews have uses beyond direct evaluation of the publications under immediate consideration. They keep the selector aware of which authors, editors, publishers, and research institutions are producing the kinds of books that will be useful to scholars, and—together with articles published in the reviewing journals—of current trends in musical scholarship. For these reasons, the selector must read book reviews widely, ideally in multiple languages.

The two most notable review sources for English-language scholarly books about music are the Music Library Association's quarterly *Notes*, and the British musicological quarterly *Music & Letters*.

*Notes.* Music Library Association, 1939–. Each quarterly issue includes about 18 to 20 in-depth reviews of books, most in English. Each issue also includes a bibliography of "Books Recently Published," based on the output of the monographic music cataloging units of the Library of Congress, described under "Print Notifications."[54]

*Music & Letters.* Oxford University Press, 1920–. Each quarterly issue typically contains about 25 in-depth reviews of important new books published in a variety of languages, mostly in English. Some issues also include an extensive review article on a narrow topic. The journal's Web site (http://ml.oxfordjournals.org/) includes a list of books reviewed in the current issue; subscribers to the journal online also have access to full text of reviews and articles. *Music & Letters* is one of the most respected international journals of music scholarship, and is renowned for its extensive review section.

Among other notable journals reviewing scholarly books on music are Ad Parnassum, American Music, Cambridge Opera Journal, Current Musicology, Dutch Journal of Music Theory, Early Music, Eighteenth-Century Music, Ethnomusicology, International Journal of Musicology, Journal of Historical Research in Music Education, Journal of Musicological Research, Journal of New Music, Journal of Seventeenth-Century Music, Journal of the American Musicological Society, Journal of the Royal Musical Association, Journal of the Society for American Music, Latin American Music Review, Music Theory Spectrum, the Musical Quarterly, Musical Opinion, the Musical Times, Die Musikforschung, MusikTheorie, Neue Zeitschrift für Musik, 19th Century Music, Nineteenth-Century Music Review, Nuova rivista musicale italiana, Opera Quarterly, Österreichische Musikzeitschrift, Philosophy of Music Education Review, Plainsong & Medieval Music, Psychology of Music, Revista de musicología, Revista musical chilena, Revue de musicologie, Rivista italiana di musicologia, Studia musicologica, Tempo, and Twentieth-Century Music.

Some of these journals have been publishing reviews for decades; others are recent additions to the musicological reviewing pantheon.

Trade books—those likely to be seen on display at Borders and Barnes & Noble stores—are usually sent to reviewers in galleys prior to publication. They are promoted to bookstores and distributors through trade publications and sold to them at deep discount (50 percent off list price is usual) with full return privileges.[55] Paragraph-length reviews of a few U.S. trade and scholarly books are found in several journals directed at library selectors and members of the book trade, such as *Choice: Current Reviews for Academic Libraries* (a searchable database of the reviews published since 1988 is ChoiceReviews.online), *Kirkus Reviews*, *Library Journal*, and *Publishers Weekly: The International News Magazine of Book Publishing*. These journals review U.S. books selectively, and thus will better serve the needs of selectors at the public library and college level than those at libraries supporting graduate research. In 2007, for example, ChoiceReviews.online reviewed just 168 music books. Most libraries subscribe to these journals in paper or online full-text, or both, and, despite the limited coverage, selectors in many subjects would do well to cast an eye over each new issue. Note also that reviews from some of these journals are reproduced on Amazon.com and Barnesandnoble.com in association with listings of the titles they have for sale.

## SELECTIVE AND ANNOTATED GUIDES

Selective guides to books about music tend not to be revised very often, if ever. The older publications listed below, therefore, must be supplemented by more recent resources for a thorough collection analysis and review.

*A Basic Music Library: Essential Scores and Books.* 2nd ed. Compiled by the Music Library Association Committee on Basic Music Collection under the direction of Pauline S. Bayne. Edited by R. Michael Fling. Chicago: ALA, 1983. This buying guide, aimed at small to medium-size libraries, lists and annotates about 550 titles in the categories of reference, periodicals and yearbooks, biographies, music theory, music history, and music of the United States. Books were dropped from the 3rd edition (1997) in favor of recommended sound recordings. At this writing, a 4th edition is in preparation; its scope and format are yet to be announced.

*Best Books for Academic Libraries.* 10 vols. Temecula, CA: The Best Books, 2002–3. Volume 9 (*Music & Fine Arts*, 2003) lists between 1,900 and 2000 music books; all appear to be U.S. publications in English, though the introduction to the set does not state the criteria for inclusion. There are no annotations. Music contributors were librarians at four major university music libraries.

Brockman, William S. *Music: A Guide to the Reference Literature.* Reference Sources in the Humanities Series. Littleton, CO: Libraries Unlimited, 1987. Contains classified and annotated listings of 560 reference works—emphasizing works in English but including historically important works in all languages—109 then-current music periodicals, and a directory of musical associations.

Brook, Barry S. and Richard Viano. *Thematic Catalogues in Music: An Annotated Bibliography.* 2nd ed. Annotated Reference Tools in Music, 5. Stuyvesant, NY: Pendragon, 1997. A bibliography of thematic catalogs, with a history of the catalogs, an annotated bibliography of works about them, and recommended guidelines for creating a catalog. Composer catalogs are entered by composer name; collective catalogs are entered by compiler name or name of library or publisher being chronicled, as appropriate to their content.

Crabtree, Phillip D. and Donald H. Foster. *Sourcebook for Research in Music.* 2nd ed. Rev. and expanded by Allen Scott. Bloomington: Indiana University Press, 2005. Intended as a textbook for graduate music students, a reference work for music faculty and professionals, and a collection evaluation and development tool for librarians. Consists of classified bibliographies of basic bibliographical tools for music research, area bibliographies and other reference sources, dictionaries and encyclopedias, sources treating the history of music, current research journals, editions of music, and miscellaneous sources. There are few annotations.

Duckles, Vincent H. and Ida Reed. *Music Reference and Research Materials: An Annotated Bibliography.* 5th ed.; Michael A. Keller, advisory editor. New York: Schirmer Books, 1997. "Duckles" has been the essential guide to music reference sources since the first edition was published in 1964. This 5th edition describes about 3,800 music reference resources published to 1995. The 399 "Bibliographies of Music Literature" listed can supplement the selective few bibliographies that are listed in this guide.

Lewis, Thomas. *The Pro/Am Guide to U.S. Books about Music: Annotated Subject Guide to Current & Backlist Titles.* White Plains, NY: Pro/Am Music Resources, 1986. Supplement, 1988. Classified list of English-language titles in print at time of its publication. Partially annotated. Includes references to reviews published in about 20 reviewing journals.

*RCL: Resources for College Libraries.* Ed. by Marcus Elmore, for the Association of College and Research Libraries. 7 vols. Chicago: ALA; New Providence, NJ: R. R. Bowker, 2006. Volume 1 ("Humanities") contains a 254-page classified bibliography of "a collection to support the study and teaching of music—the music of all peoples, places, and times, in all its historical, cultural, technical, and critical dimensions—at an undergraduate level. Emphasis is on current and recent scholarship, with some classic works included for historical depth even when subsequent writings have superseded them. Textbooks and popular-level books are excluded except when indispensable as introductions to the topic. Notated scores and recorded performances (audio or video) are excluded except as an integral supplement to a book" (headnote to the music section, by Kent Underwood, music subject editor for the set, and music librarian at New York University). This set is successor to the 3rd edition of *Books for College Libraries* (1988).

## PUBLISHERS

A number of scholarly and trade publishers in the United States are known for issuing important books about music. Among these are university presses, some of which have extensive catalogs of such titles; these include, but are not limited to, presses of the universities of California, Cambridge, Chicago, Columbia, Cornell, Duke, Harvard, Indiana, Massachusetts Institute of Technology, Michigan, Nebraska, Oxford, Princeton, Rochester, Yale, and Wesleyan.[56] Other university presses issue occasional music titles of primarily regional interest. A number of other publishers, though lacking the cachet of a university imprimatur, also bring out books that medium-to-large-size libraries will find to be essential additions to their music collections. Take note particularly of the following presses in the United States:

Amadeus Press, http://www.amadeuspress.com/

Ashgate Publishing, http://www.ashgate.com/

Da Capo Books, http://www.perseusbooksgroup.com/
  dacapo/home.jsp

W. W. Norton & Company, http://www.wwnorton.com/

Pendragon Press, http://www.pendragonpress.com/

Routledge, http://www.routledge.com/

Scarecrow Press, http://www.scarecrowpress.com/

Schirmer Reference, http://www.gale.com/schirmer/

# PRICES

The Music Library Association publishes an annual summary of "Prices of Music Monographs and Scores as Reflected in *Notes*" in each December issue of its journal. According to this survey, the average price in 2006 for 1,237 monographs with an imprint of 2004 or later was $46.33. Average prices were also derived for principal languages: English ($47.91), French ($36.99), German ($56.81), Italian ($32.93), and Spanish ($23.44). The compiler of the column notes that the figures are "intended to show general trends in pricing of music materials, and should be used only as a guide to collection-development planning."[57] The *Bowker Annual* of 2007 posted an average price for U.S. music books published in 2006 as $56.51. Prices for the 838 titles added to the Theodore Front database in 2007 ranged from a low of $5.95 to a high of $1,295, with an average price of $59.87.

# Periodicals

The earliest music periodical is generally acknowledged to be *Critica musica* (1722–25) by Johann Mattheson, who contributed all of the content. "Modern" music periodicals —with content from multiple authors—arose at the conclusion of the eighteenth century, the first being the *Allgemeine musikalische Zeitung*, published in Leipzig by Breitkopf & Härtel from 1798 through 1865. *The Euterpiad, or Musical Intelligencer* (1820–23), which reported news primarily of Boston musical life is considered the first true music periodical published in the United States.

## PUBLISHING OUTPUT

From Mattheson's beginnings in 1722 to the year 2000, some 9,259 music periodicals were published.[58] In May 2008, the online database of *Ulrich's Periodicals Directory* (UlrichsWeb.com, http://www.ulrichsweb.com/)— containing bibliographic information on a quarter-million publications from more than 130,000 publishers in 200 countries—listed 3,160 active titles with the subject "music." UlrichsWeb.com divided these into the categories of "Academic/Scholarly" (707 titles), "Consumer" (1,116), "Newsletter/Bulletin" (396), "Newspaper" (48), and "Trade/Business-to-Business" (265), leaving 628 titles escaping categorization. Of the total, 1,964 were in English. These numbers are inflated by the inclusion of an undetermined number of monographic series, whose components would normally be cataloged as individual books or as sets. In addition, periodicals that are published in both paper and electronic formats are listed by Ulrich's twice.

A more realistic accounting of the numbers of music periodicals being published today is likely to be found at the indexing and abstracting services. *RILM Abstracts of Music Literature* has been fully citing, indexing, and abstracting music literature in all formats since 1967. In May 2008, RILM's online version (at http://www.rilm.org/journals.html) listed 746 primary journal titles then being indexed, 372 of which it categorized as "core" (devoted completely to music scholarship, and therefore abstracted thoroughly). At that same time, the International Index to Music Periodicals (IIMP) listed 440 titles being indexed; IIMP's sister International Index to Music Periodicals Full Text (IIMPFT) listed 133 titles indexed (a spreadsheet showing title lists and chronological coverage of both versions is at http://iimp.chadwyck.com/marketing/titles.jsp). The Music Index Online since 1975 has indexed a total of 823 music periodical titles; in May 2008, 392 titles were being actively indexed (title list is at http://www .harmonieparkpress.com/Mindex.asp). Regarding currency and overlap among these indexes, see "Indexing and Abstracting Services" below for comments from a study published in 2001 comparing them.

In 1999, Lois Kuyper-Rushing published the results of a dissertation citation study that sought to identify core journals for music collections.[59] She based her findings on the bibliographies in 118 dissertations in the disciplines of musicology, music theory, music education, applied music, ethnomusicology, conducting, music therapy, and piano pedagogy. While her resulting lists are relatively short (nine to thirty-three titles, depending upon the discipline), libraries that support training in these disciplines might find this article a useful starting point in reviewing their subscription lists.

Today's music periodicals may focus on composers, instruments, vocal music, recordings, popular music, jazz, education, bibliography, music of a particular genre or era, theory, or musicology. Depending upon their subject emphasis, they may contain research articles; reviews of books, scores, recordings, and performances; bibliographies and discographies; news of current and forthcoming events; interviews; lists and advertisements of new publications; and opinion pieces and letters to the editor. Some music periodicals are published in online as well as print format, and a few are available *only* online, in some cases at no charge.

Representative English-language periodicals are American Music, American Record Guide, Cambridge Opera Journal, Early Music, Eighteenth Century Music, Ethnomusicology, Gramophone, International Journal of Music Education, Journal of Music Theory, Journal of Research in Music Education, Journal of the American Musicological Society, Journal of the Society for American Music, Latin American Music Review, Music Educators Journal, Musical Quarterly, Musical Times, 19th Century Music, Music Analysis, Music & Letters, Notes, Opera News, Perspectives of New Music, Popular Music, and Tempo. Some of these titles are the products of music associations and societies. Academic and research libraries typically also subscribe to periodicals in languages other than English.

## KEEPING CURRENT WITH PERIODICALS

A prime source of information about new periodicals is the semiannual "New Periodicals" column in the Music Library Association's journal *Notes*. This column "selectively lists newly issued periodicals; describes their objectives, formats, and contents; and provides information about special issues, title and format changes, mergers, and cessations."[60]

Librarians with access to the online UlrichsWeb.com can execute "advanced" searches for journals with the subject "music" and a particular startup year or range of years, producing a list of new, recent, or contemporaneous periodical launches. These searches can be limited to refereed journals by language, country of publication, and other features. A modified search can also provide a list of music journals recently ceased, to assist in cleanup of the library's subscription list. At the Ulrich's site, one also can register to receive Magazines for Libraries Update, a quarterly e-mail service dedicated to the review and analysis of journals of note that have been published since the most recent edition of the annual *Magazines for Libraries* (see below).

## SELECTIVE AND ANNOTATED GUIDES

Basart, Ann P. *Writing About Music: A Guide to Publishing Opportunities for Authors and Reviewers*. Fallen Leaf Reference Books in Music, 11. Berkeley, CA: Fallen Leaf Press, 1989. A bibliography of over 430 music journals active in the late 1980s, from 21 countries, that then were publishing "serious, informative, music-related articles and/or reviews in English. . . . Covers a large spectrum of periodicals—some scholarly and rigorous, some practical and informal, some aimed at a wide audi-

ence, some extremely specialized. The fields covered . . . include concert music, country music, popular music, folk music, ethnic music,
opera, liturgical music, film music, choral music; bands and orchestras, instruments and instrumental music; music education; musicology and ethnomusicology; record and audio equipment; electronic
and computer music; the history and theory of music; analysis and
composition; psychology of music and music therapy. Also included
are publications devoted to individual composers and performers (excluding pop music fanzines). Some interdisciplinary journals
(for example, those in the fields of arts management, arts medicine,
aesthetics, acoustics, history, and criticism) will also be found here"
(p. xi). Gives detailed information about focus, types of articles and
reviews published (with examples cited), circulation size, manuscript
mechanics, whether refereed—essentially, everything the potential
author, reviewer, or subscriber would want to know.

Fellinger, Imogen, et al. "Periodicals" (rev. 29 July 2003). Grove Music
Online, http://www.grovemusic.com/. The Grove list of 9,259 titles
"provides information on musical periodicals from the earliest such
publication (1722) to the end of the 20th century. It includes yearbooks
and almanacs on music and the annual reports of musical institutions.
Though intended as comprehensive, the list does not claim to be complete. Art, theatre and other general cultural periodicals containing
musical sections, as well as journals in other fields closely related to
music such as acoustics and liturgy, are included selectively according
to their musical significance up to about 1900, as are 20th-century periodicals on recording, jazz, rock and pop. Musical periodicals published
as supplements to newspapers or non-musical periodicals are named
only when they are of special importance. Excluded are publicity and
sale sheets from music publishers, concert guides and programs, directories and periodicals of fan clubs, reports of congresses, periodical
*Festschriften* (special honorary issues), monograph series and series
containing collections of essays, and periodical publications of music"
(exclusions stated in introduction to the list). Arranged geographically,
with a title index. Entries are not annotated.

Fidler, Linda M. and Richard S. James, eds. *International Music Journals.*
Historical Guides to the World's Periodicals and Newspapers. New
York: Greenwood Press, 1990. A bibliography of 181 of "the leading

journals throughout the many music professions, [conceived] as a thoroughly international and cross-disciplinary guide, and it includes titles of historical as well a contemporary significance. In addition to journals representing the traditional fields of music scholarship (musicology, ethnomusicology, theory, therapy, education, and their subcategories), publications important in performance, composition, popular music, discography, and librarianship are included" (p. xiv). There is a detailed publication history for each title, and sources for further information. The volume's introduction provides a concise history of music periodicals. Any music collection that aspires to be of "research" caliber should endeavor to subscribe to, or to acquire, all of these titles. In April 2007, 33 of the 181 were available in full-text at JSTOR (Journal STORage: The Scholarly Journal Archive),[61] with others surely to be added subsequently. Many of these are also available through various aggregators, and as reprints and in microform.

*Magazines for Libraries.* New York: Bowker, 1969–. Annual since 2002. This publication profiles top-rated periodicals, including general-interest magazines, research journals, and high-quality commercial publications suitable for a range of libraries in public, academic, special, government, and school settings (see the publisher's description at http://www.bowker.com/catalog/000054.htm). The 2008 edition's "Music" section—compiled by three music librarians and a public-services librarian—listed 106 current, recommended titles: of these, 58 are "general" titles published mainly in the United States and Europe, 31 are on "popular" musical topics of interest to both academics and general audiences, and 17 focus primarily on reviews of classical recorded music and audio equipment. Magazines for Libraries Update, a quarterly e-mail service dedicated to the review and analysis of journals of note that have been published since the most recent edition of the print volume, is available for free subscription at the UlrichsWeb. com site (http://www.ulrichsweb.com/ulrichsweb/). It is not possible to limit this update service to particular subjects.

Robinson, Doris. *Music and Dance Periodicals: An International Directory & Guidebook.* Voorheesville, NY: Peri Press, 1989. "An annotated listing by subject of some 1,867 currently published periodicals. It is intended to provide comprehensive coverage of the music and dance periodical field" (p. vii). Indexed by title, publisher and organization, subject, country of publication, and ISSN.

# INDEXING AND ABSTRACTING SERVICES

There are four principal indexing services for music research. Répertoire international de la presse musicale (RIPM) is an ongoing project to index early—primarily nineteenth-century—music journals.[62] Music Index Online, RILM Abstracts, and International Index to Music Periodicals focus on indexing current literature; these three are moving targets in terms of indexing depth and overlap, extent of international coverage, types of journals indexed, currency of coverage, and amount of retrospective indexing. A survey of the three, published in 2001, is the most recent as of this writing.[63] The authors of the survey concluded that, because of

> the varying degree of currency, the low degree of overlapping periodical titles and the . . . selectivity of indexing, . . . it appears that major research libraries have little choice but to subscribe to all three databases, simply as insurance against their collective weaknesses. . . . Music librarians without sufficient funds to subscribe to all three must carefully weigh the strengths and weaknesses of each database, but with the realization that they will not have access to a considerable portion of the music periodical literature.[64]

Not exactly ringing endorsements.

The following descriptions are based on mid-2008 claims made by the services on their Web sites; Troutman and Green concluded, in their analyses of IIMP, Music Index Online, and RILM, that these claims tend to be less than precise.

**International Index to Music Periodicals: IIMP,** http://iimp.chadwyck.com/marketing/about.jsp. Indexing was begun in 1996, but it includes much retrospective information. Indexes about 430 journals published in over 20 countries in 17 languages. Includes over 530,000 records, a large proportion of which index the most recent eight years of publication. More than 200,000 are from backfiles (up to 1995); many commence at the first issues of journals' runs, some starting as early as 1874. IIMP includes a comprehensive range of subject areas in both scholarly and popular music journals (a title list and dates of coverage are posted at the Web site). In addition to journal articles, citations are included for reviews, conference papers, program descriptions, concert reviews, and recordings if they are of scholarly interest. Updated monthly. IIMP Full Text, a version with full text of around 110 core music journals, is available by separate subscription. Both versions are available from ProQuest Information & Learning. Available free to subscribers of IIMP *or* IIMP Full Text and to subscribers of IIPA *or* IIPA Full Text is Music & Performing Arts Online, a portal that searches both resources simultaneously.

**Music Index Online,** http://www.harmonieparkpress.com/MusicIndex .asp. This is the granddaddy of music periodical indexes. The print version dates from 1949, and online coverage begins with 1974. Indexes more than 850 periodicals from over 40 countries in 22 languages, with more than one million records online. Covers classical and popular music in all styles and genres. Cited are book reviews, obituaries, new periodicals, and news and articles about music, musicians, and the music industry. The print version has quarterly supplements, cumulated annually in one or two print volumes. Available online through Harmonie Park Press and EBSCO.[65]

**RILM Abstracts of Music Literature,** http://www.rilm.org/ (Print publication began in 1967). Unlike IIMP and Music Index Online, RILM's horizon stretches beyond periodicals. "All scholarly works are included: articles, books, bibliographies, catalogues, dissertations, Festschriften, films and videos, iconographies, critical commentaries to complete works, ethnographic recordings, conference proceedings, electronic resources, and reviews." RILM's list of primary journal titles as posted on its Web site distinguishes between "core" journals that are indexed and abstracted thoroughly, and those that are treated selectively. As of this writing, the database contains over 400,000 entries, with about 30,000 added each year. Unlike the preceding two indexes, which are purely U.S.-based commercial enterprises, RILM (like RIPM, described below) is a cooperative undertaking by an international network of institutions and scholars, functioning under the auspices of the International Musicological Society, and the International Association of Music Libraries, Archives, and Documentation Centres. The online version is available with monthly updates through CSA, EBSCO, NISC, OCLC, and Ovid. A CD-ROM version available from NISC is updated quarterly, and a print version from the RILM International Center is published annually. RILM and RIPM complement each other in terms of chronological coverage, and subscribers to both can search them simultaneously online.

Répertoire international de la presse musicale: RIPM, http://www.ripm
.org/. Indexes mostly nineteenth-century music periodicals. Coverage
has recently been extended to include periodicals that ceased publication before or around 1950. At this writing, contains more than 525,000
annotated citations (including more than 250,000 reviews and 11,500
biographical citations) from over 100 titles published in 15 countries,
published in more than 220 print volumes, with 10 new volumes
added per year. RIPM—as is RILM, above—is a cooperative undertaking by an international network of institutions and scholars, functioning under the auspices of the International Musicological Society, and
the International Association of Music Libraries, Archives, and Documentation Centres. The online database, which is available through
EBSCO, NISC, OCLC, and Ovid, is updated semiannually; RIPM in
print and on CD-ROM are available from NISC. RIPM and RILM
(above) complement each other in terms of chronological coverage,
and subscribers to both can search them simultaneously online.[66]

## PRICES

Music periodical subscription costs are, generally speaking, lower than for
most other disciplines, and have had lower inflation rates. In the *Bowker
Annual*, the table of "U.S. Periodicals: Average Prices and Price Indexes,
2004–2006" confirms this, to a certain extent.[67] The average cost in 2007
of "Fine and applied arts" periodicals (corresponding to Library of Congress classes M and N—Bowker has no separate "Music" category) was
$77.63. Only "Children's periodicals," "General interest periodicals" and
"Physical education and recreation" posted lower average costs. The table
also showed that only the first two of these three categories had lower cost
increases since 1984. Although these calculations do not include the many
popular British periodicals found in U.S. music collections—*Gramophone*,
*BBC Music Magazine*, *Early Music*, and *Music & Letters*, for example—or
important and widely subscribed ones from other countries, they are probably indicative of broader trends.

Periodical subscription payments by an actual music library, reflecting
what academic libraries tend to collect, may be more informative than figures for some U.S. totality. In fiscal year 2005–6, the average paid per title

for 286 subscriptions to paper and e-journals by Indiana University's Cook Music Library, whose data the author was able to access, was $86.42. This did not include annual payments for electronic databases, audio streaming, and indexing services—Classical Music Library, Naxos Music Library, International Index to Music Periodicals, Music Index Online, RILM Abstracts, and Grove Music Online—which collectively during that fiscal year accounted for 40.7 percent of this library's total paid subscriptions. Neither did it include titles on subscription that, for whatever reason, were not invoiced during that fiscal year.

# *Selection Strategies*

## COLLECTION DEVELOPMENT POLICIES

Many collection development librarians consider written collection policies to be indispensable preludes to effective selection. Collection policies, they say, explain to users the library's goals and objectives, translate them into specific guidelines for subjects and types of materials to be acquired, and defend the library from, or provide it with a system for responding to, individuals and organizations who want to remove "offensive" material (explicit lyrics in pop music, for example, continue to be targets of would-be censors).

Some skeptics argue that collection policies at best provide a snapshot of collection scope, subjects, users, formats, and other mutable selection criteria, fixing those elements in a matrix that is unresponsive to the changing realities of scholarship and publication. While the academic selector will have guidance from a documented music curriculum outlining the requirements of its primary users, what of the music-related needs in other areas: anthropology, comparative literature, film studies, and the like?

Whatever one's personal position, it is a near certainty that at some point a library's administration will involve the music selector in writing or revising a collection policy. In this situation, a template is likely to come down from on high, and selectors will be expected to insert information relative to their disciplines. If the music selector should have a freer hand, however, the following guide can be useful in developing a collection policy from scratch.

Amanda Maple and Jean Morrow. *Guide to Writing Collection Development Policies for Music.* Music Library Association Technical Reports, 26. Lanham, MD: Scarecrow, for the Music Library Association, 2001.

This guide was commissioned by the MLA Resource Sharing and Collection Development Committee. The authors adapted the format of ALA's *Guide for Written Collection Policy Statements* (2nd ed., 1996), and *Reference Collection Development: A Manual* (1992).[68] The guide includes a checklist for writing a music policy; an outline for a specimen policy, with examples contributed by twelve college, university, conservatory, and public libraries; the complete text of the policy from Middlebury College Music Library; a glossary; and a selected bibliography.

## EIGHT COLLECTION-BUILDING OBJECTIVES

The following eight collection-building objectives are perhaps the minimum to which a large music library should aspire.[69] Smaller libraries may be able to modify these objectives to meet more modest local needs.

1. Collect serious new books and current journals about music (in print and/or electronic format), in English as well as designated foreign languages, covering serious as well as popular and world musics and revised editions of older books, paying attention particularly to what is required for curricular support.

   Focus on current materials to build archives for future scholarship. Prices for new publications will never be lower (though reprints in paperback of scholarly books are common after a few years of solid sales in hardback), and what is new today may be out of print tomorrow.

2. Collect well-edited practical editions of standard musical repertoire, of "new" music likely to be performed widely, and good recorded performances in both categories. Collect recordings of popular and world music in support of identified research and instruction needs.

   Identifying newly-composed music expected to be of lasting worth requires a leap of faith (a library school diploma does not come with a crystal ball). Clues abound, however, for the attentive librarian. New works issued by major print publishers—a Boosey & Hawkes or a Bärenreiter, for example—have already, to a large extent, been vetted for their artistic value. Composers and works commissioned by well-known performers and organizations will attract immediate attention, and are potentially of continuing interest. Composers who win awards and prizes are already recognized for their excellence (see the chapter on awards for descriptions of major composition prizes), and new works that achieve uniformly excellent reviews in their concert and recorded realizations ought to attract the attention of the selector. To stay aware of these trends, the librarian must keep abreast of news and events in the music world (see the following section on "Keeping Current" for some helpful online and print resources for this purpose). Input from local composers and performers of new music should also be sought.

3. Collect scholarly critical editions and facsimiles (print, microform, and digital image files) for study of earlier music of recognized musical worth, including monumental sets and *Denkmäler.*

   These are usually classified by Library of Congress as M2, and composers' collected editions as M3.

4. Collect pedagogical and etude works to meet *identified* needs of users, not to serve in place of what students need to buy for themselves, but as exemplars in support of courses that teach instructional methods.

   Syllabi from these courses should be consulted, or advice sought from their instructors.

5. Collect materials to meet local research and performance needs (faculty research, dissertations, etc.).

   While the library should not be expected to purchase performance materials for a school's large ensembles (orchestra, band, choirs), scores and recordings of works being prepared for performance by these groups will be of interest to library users.

6. Collect materials documenting local and regional music, including printed and recorded editions of works by local researchers, composers, and performers.

   Academic libraries have tended to interpret this narrowly to mean music of their own institutions, in the expectation that the public library will take up the slack. A more catholic approach is to be encouraged.

7. Collect anything *beyond* what is mentioned above in order to fulfill obligations in any consortial or other cooperative agreements.

8. Provide for removal of superseded editions *if desired.*

   Research libraries tend to maintain historical collections to enable the curious to examine earlier research and editorial practices, including those no longer in fashion. If shelf space is limited, these may be candidates for remote storage.

## KEEPING CURRENT

Keeping current about goings-on in the classical music world is essential for the librarian who selects printed and recorded new music. *Tempo: A Quarterly Review of Modern Music* is one of the most systematic among music journals in its coverage of new music. Each issue includes, in addition to reviews of first performances, a "News Section" that lists, in a straightforward exposition by composers' names, the most recent commissions, premieres, and awards and prizes. Another print source of news is the "Here & There" column in the bimonthly *American Record Guide*, which is a staple in many libraries (*American Record Guide* took up the mantle of music news provider that was laid down by *Musical America* when it ceased publication in 1992).

A primary source for industry news is the weekly *Billboard*—available in print and online versions—which has been required reading for persons in the music trades since 1894; although its focus is on popular music (*Billboard*'s pop "charts" document music sales and radio play), classical music and jazz are also covered to a lesser extent. Other journals also contain news sections, often tailored for a particular musical readership; for this reason, it is a good idea for the music selector to scan all new journal issues that come into the library for news stories, in addition to the ads, reviews, and other features.

Several music Web sites feature articles, reviews of recordings and performances, interviews, and other news of the music world. Those listed below offer online registration for free e-mail updates and newsletters.

**American Music Center,** http://www.amc.net/. This important resource about new American music has a link to NewMusicBox (http://www .newmusicbox.org/), a "Web-based advocacy magazine and portal dedicated to the music of American composers and improvisers and their champions. A multi-media publication from the American Music Center, NewMusicBox offers: in-depth articles and discussions; up-to-the-minute industry news and commentary; coverage of upcoming performances, new books and recordings; plus on-demand concert webcasts." Online visitors can register to receive the center's monthly e-newsletter *AMC eNotes*, as well as e-mail updates to NewMusicBox.

**ArtsJournal.com,** http://www.artsjournal.com/. "The daily digest of arts, culture & ideas." Subscription is free for the daily or weekly *ArtsJournal Free*, which provides links to arts stories worldwide. Paid subscription to *ArtsJournal Premium* adds descriptive content, and can be limited to general arts stories (daily), and/or weekly music, theater, and visual-arts reports.

**BBC Music,** http://www.bbc.co.uk/music/. Featured are music news items and CD reviews. In addition to classical music, this site has areas devoted to jazz, blues/soul/reggae, classic pop/rock, world, and other musical genres. Visitors to the site can register to receive a weekly e-mail newsletter about one or more of these musical genres.

**BBC Music Magazine,** http://www.bbcmusicmagazine.com/. Contains information about the current, past, and future print issues of the journal, and a searchable international calendar of concert listings. Registration for the free e-mail newsletter also provides access to the journal's online CD reviews archive.

**Gramophone,** http://www.gramophone.co.uk/. Online news and features about classical music, based primarily on content from the print journal of the same title, and a link to Gramofile, the free, full-text, searchable archive of CD reviews published in the journal. "Online Journals" features weekly reports from *Gramophone* correspondents around the world. A moderated online chat forum posts reader commentary, and its archive is searchable. A monthly e-mail newsletter is sent on request.

**Music Academy Online,** http://www.musicacademyonline.com/. Music news categories include "Recent Headlines," "Ensemble and Performer News," "Composer News," "Events and Festivals," "Reviews," and "Staff Favorites." Updated daily. Editorial articles are published at irregular intervals. Registration for e-mail news updates is available.

MusicalAmerica.com, http://musicalamerica.com/. This online successor to the defunct print journal *Musical America* includes news articles in the categories of "People in the News," "Contests & Awards," "Reviews," and "Reader Comments." The site editor selects news articles from Associated Press wires, and there are additional submissions from international correspondents, including reviews from music critics in cities around the world. Updated daily. Full access is by paid subscription, but registration for the weekly e-mail newsletter, access to press releases, and a calendar of events is free.

## FOUR TYPES OF SELECTION TOOLS

There are four general categories of selection tools for music materials. Depending upon the format being selected (books, scores, recordings, journals), they are of varying value and utility.

1. *Mailings from publishers.* These typically take the form of mailed announcements of new and recent books or scores. A way to get on these mailing lists is to join the Music Library Association, and other music organizations such as the American Musicological Society, Society for Ethnomusicology, Society for Music Theory, and College Music Society, all of which rent their mailing lists to publishers and other organizations interested in informing potential customers about new publications.

   Many publishers also have "request a catalog" options on their Web sites, or enable signup for e-mail updates about new publications in focused areas of interest. Few publishers any longer go to the expense of printing complete catalogs, considering the more economical alternative of Web publication, though there are a few holdouts. A valuable resource for monitoring catalog availability is the quarterly "Music Publishers' Catalogs" column in MLA's *Notes*, compiled for many years by George R. Hill. It lists all catalogs received by Hill since the previous issue, and aims at comprehensive coverage. "Also included are stock order blanks, agents' catalogs, catalogs of books on music, catalogs of single series, substantial publishers' catalogs of single composers, and rental catalogs. Excluded are catalogs that are exclusively retail. The list also includes catalogs published by national music centers and by licensing agencies" (headnote to the column). During 2007, a total of 386 catalogs, varying in size from a single leaf to 328 pages, were listed. The music selector will find it useful to monitor this column, and to request catalogs of interest that may not have been mailed automatically (mailing addresses and URLs are provided for this purpose). Although the catalogs that publishers post on their Web sites have their utility, many of them are not easily browsable, whereas a print catalog can be a pleasure to scan.

2. *Mailings from vendors.* Because libraries are vendors' platelets and plasma, you can be sure that vendors are making their best efforts to keep library selectors up-to-date about new and forthcoming publications. Depending upon the vendor, notifications might include *all* new and relevant music titles known to the vendor, or be limited to such titles as fit a profile prepared by the library, and may be delivered in paper format or as direct e-mails. Alternatively, vendors' databases allow the librarian to check in when convenient, and view online all relevant titles added there in a preceding month, or other period defined by the librarian. (Notification services of particular vendors are described elsewhere in this guide.)

3. *Journal advertisements, reviews, new-publications lists, bibliographies, etc.* A variety of types of selection information comes into libraries in magazines, newsletters, and journals. These can inform of both new publications (in reviews, lists of publications submitted for review, advertisements, and the like) and older publications for potential retrospective purchase (special-subject bibliographies, literature surveys, and so forth). The committed music selector will do a preliminary examination of *all* new journal issues as they come into the library, setting aside for closer examination those that have substantial reviews and ad copy. One quickly learns which titles have regular, useful selection features, and which do not, making triage almost second nature as the selector gains experience.

4. *National and trade bibliographies.* Coverage of books about music in these bibliographies is comprehensive, and published with sufficient frequency to make them practical for selection purposes. Although it is unlikely that a music library would

subscribe to any bibliographies that cover books on all subjects, most academic and public libraries have provisions to circulate new issues of "professional" journals to selectors who express interest in examining them. In the United States, the monthly *American Book Publishing Record* lists, with full cataloging data, all of the new trade and scholarly books published, arranged by Dewey classification for easy scanning of music books in the 780s. *Publishers' Weekly*, directed at the book trade, includes industry news, interviews, and advertisements, as well as short reviews of forthcoming books that are expected to be of interest to browsers at bookstores. National and trade bibliographies of other countries can also be of interest to selectors of books. The weekly *British National Bibliography*, the weekly *Deutsche Nationalbibliographie* of German-language books, and the monthly *Les livres du mois* of French-language texts are among the most useful in this respect. Several countries also produce national bibliographies of printed music; these are described in the "Printed Music" chapter.

## SELECTION DECISIONS

Selection of printed and recorded music often involves a series of yes-or-no decisions so complex as to defy deconstruction (a flowchart could go on for pages). In addition to the usual factors of budget, relevance to curriculum, and other local needs, the music selector might have to consider the following elements when deciding whether or not to order an edition. A negative response to any *one* of these criteria can send a title to the reject pile.

**Composer.** Composers of the musical canon—the "Three Bs" of Bach, Beethoven, and Brahms, for example—pose little for the selector to think about in terms of the music's intrinsic value. Early composers of lesser stature, on the other hand—the Martinis, Marpurgs, and Matthesons— may require a judicious choice between what is wanted for the sake of collection comprehensiveness, and what the budget can bear. As music notation software makes editing and producing them simpler and more economical, and as early-music performers rummage through the works of the *Kleinmeistern* for new repertoire, increasing numbers of such composers' works are being published.

Selectors of twentieth- and twenty-first-century composers must give attention to music news, events, and reviews (discussed elsewhere in this guide) as a way of evaluating these composers' current reputations and potential staying power. Use of a list of worthy composers of "new" music, developed in consultation with faculty colleagues and reviewed regularly, can make selection of new printed and recorded editions of their works virtually automatic. Vendors that service approval plans for printed music have developed extensive lists of these composers; these lists can serve as starting points for developing a more selective local list (see the discussion of approval plans, below).

**Editor.** Experts who write about a composer's or a "school's" works may also edit them for scholarly publication; several works by nineteenth-century composer Felix Mendelssohn, for example, have been edited for publication by John Michael Cooper, who also has written extensively about the composer. Similarly, many performers specialize in the preparation of practical editions of solo and chamber music for particular instruments (see virtuoso Janos Starker's editions for the cello). After time spent perusing new issues of journals arriving in the library, the selector will become familiar with the specialties and reputations of many editors and use their work to inform purchasing decisions.

**Publisher.** Publishers acquire reputations, just as editors do. See the discussion of printed-music and book publishers elsewhere in this guide for descriptions of a few of them.

**Edition.** There seems always to be a market for new editions of standard repertoire; otherwise, publishers would simply reprint the old ones. Newly discovered sources, and re-interpretation of older ones in light of recent scholarship, often make the re-editing of these works a worthwhile endeavor. Familiarity with the publisher and editor can help the selector decide whether or not to purchase a new edition of a work already owned in other editions. Sometimes, such editions are extracts for the use of performers from composers' scholarly collected editions. Often, however, the question is as simple as "Do we really need *another* edition of this?" Checking the circulation frequency of the work in editions already owned by the library—today's integrated online systems have made this a simple task—can nudge the selector in one or the other direction.

**Instrumentation or genre.** An institution's curriculum may limit or support the need to acquire music for particular instruments or genres. If a school has no jazz program, there may be little local interest in or need for the "fake" books and improvisation instruction manuals that are published in large numbers, or for a comprehensive collection of jazz recordings. Similarly, if the institution offers no guitar instruction, there may be little need to acquire guitar music beyond a core collection. The school's course catalog will list the relevant areas of instruction, and the correlation of selection to curriculum should also be recognized in a written collection policy, if there is one.

**Format.** An edition may be offered in multiple formats, depending upon the performance medium. Full (conductor's) score, miniature (study) score, score together with performance parts for chamber music, parts alone, and vocal score (instrumental accompaniment reduced for piano) are among the formats most frequently encountered. A library at a conservatory or comprehensive school of music will likely want to acquire performance parts, when available, in addition to the scores of chamber music works, but a library at an academic music department that does not offer performance instruction may have no need to purchase performance parts. However, all possible formats for a particular work may not be offered for sale. A string quartet by a contemporary composer may be offered only in score format, necessitating rental of the string parts by groups that want to perform it. On the other hand, many chamber works are published only as sets, with score and parts delivered as a unit. A library wanting to acquire a work sometimes must settle for whatever format is available, whether or not it suits its typical user's needs.

**Audience.** Editions intended for beginning instrumentalists may not be of interest to a library at a university or conservatory, where advanced students are trained. Music publishers' catalogs, and the editions themselves, sometimes carry grading symbols to indicate the level of performance difficulty—commonly a five- or seven-step system with "1" indicating the work is for beginning students, and "5" or "7" for advanced ones, though other schemes exist. The level may also be described verbally, and not necessarily in English. French editions, for example, may be designated as *facile* (easy), *moyenne difficulté* (medium difficulty), and the like. Vendors may also provide notes in their announcements to describe the level of difficulty, or the intended audience for the edition being offered.

A parallel situation exists for music *books* intended for young readers. Books cataloged by the Library of Congress that are intended for young people usually have a "Juvenile literature" subdivision in the subject headings, if the selector is working with LC cataloging copy. But the target audience might not otherwise be clear from the bibliographic description. Many of us have unwittingly ordered a promising title by a respected author—such as *Mozart* by Percy M. Young, a biographer of Edward Elgar, George Grove, and Arthur Sullivan—only to receive a small picture-book for children.

**Language.** Libraries may formally declare in a collection development policy in what languages they collect. This is rather straightforward in the case of books, but selectors must beware of texts originally written and published in English, but newly translated into another language that also is collected by the library. What is the librarian to do, however, in the case of an opera composed and traditionally sung in Russian, now being offered in a printed vocal score with no interlinear English "singing" translation; or a recorded song cycle sung in the original German, but lacking English program notes and vocal text translations? The selector's decision may depend upon what alternative editions may be available, in addition to the other criteria discussed here.

**Date.** Publishers sometimes reprint scores with no significant change other than a new date on the title page, just as book publishers may reprint in paperback a title previously issued in hardback. The existence of an earlier copyright date on the edition, or in an OCLC WorldCat cataloging record, can be a clue. Be aware also that scores may first appear in print several years *after* the "publication" date shown on the item and in the vendor's announcement; this gap in time is fairly common in the case of works originally "published" for distribution by rental, but newly offered for sale.

**Reissue/Reprint.** Many recorded performances are reissued, sometimes multiple times, either by their original labels (RCA Victor has reissued Toscanini's 1952 Carnegie Hall recording of Beethoven's Symphony no. 9 no fewer than twelve times), or by different labels (Maria Callas's "Lisbon" *Traviata*, recorded live in 1958, has appeared on at least five labels). Regardless of the label, reissues typically have new accompanying material (program notes and translations) and may include modified content (coupled with different repertoire, for example). Reviewing media usually note when a recording is a reissue, and what revisions there may be in the new version. It is then up to the selector to decide whether this newly reissued performance would actually be "new" to the library.

Also, printed music editions are sometimes reborn; the reprint publishers identified in the "Printed Music" chapter are in the business of resurrecting the public-domain out-of-print editions of other publishers. But publishers may also reprint their own editions, sometimes in a different format to appeal to a different audience. Henle Verlag, for example, has released individual piano sonatas extracted from its collected critical edition of the *Werke* of Joseph Haydn; the same editions show up in a volume of *selected* Haydn sonatas from Henle, in its paperbound three-volume set of all the piano sonatas by Haydn, and in a study-score edition of the sonatas. Binding, size, and prefatory material may be changed, but the music itself is not.

**Sets/Series.** The selector must be continually aware of the ongoing sets and series being received on standing orders (used for publications that appear in successive volumes or parts, and for which the library expects to pay for each as it is received). Heading off the inadvertent firm order (used for publications for which the library expects to pay only once) for a new title in one of these series is a constant challenge. It is convenient for this purpose to have a regularly updated list of the library's standing orders close at hand when considering a new title that is part of a series.

**Price.** Each library will define its own criteria, which can vary depending upon the type of publication. Expect to pay top dollar for critical editions and color facsimiles, for example. The library will certainly be influenced by the state of the materials budget during the course of the fiscal year. Fluctuating currency-exchange rates are also a factor, since many important music editions are published abroad (among the convenient currency-exchange utilities available online is XE.com Universal Currency Converter, http://www.xe.com/ucc/).

With the advent of online catalogs and databases, pre-order searches and verification of titles selected for potential acquisition have become much easier. Still, the particular reasons for a selection remain as complex as ever, due to factors already described. Many music selectors, therefore, will find it expedient to do pre-order searching themselves, rather than passing the task along to an assistant who may not be aware of the thought processes behind each selection or know whether alternate editions or versions will be acceptable for addition to the collection.

## APPROVAL PLANS

Music selectors who are daunted by the planning process can arrange to have someone else do at least part the work for them. Approval plans have been used for decades as a way to acquire some of the materials that would have been firm-ordered anyway. [70] The library creates a profile describing what is needed, and places it with a vendor who monitors the output of hundreds of publishers, then sends the library new editions that match its profile. Titles that the library judges to be unsatisfactory can be returned to the vendor for credit. Book approval plans have been justified as a way to save library staff time, and to aid in the building of a core collection. For music collections, however, another possible reason to use approval plans might be that the required musical knowledge can be thin on the ground in all but the best-staffed libraries. A library with only one or two music specialists can expect that much of their time will be consumed by answering reference inquiries, giving bibliographic instruction, managing staff, performing committee responsibilities, maintaining relationships with music faculty, and the like. But building a music collection hands-on can be a full-time job. In libraries employing several music librarians, the work may be parceled out among them, one being responsible for selecting printed music, one for recorded music, and one for books and periodicals, for example. In smaller establishments, approval plans can be an efficient way to bring in much of what is needed without overburdening the music selector.

Many music librarians in academic settings benefit from library-wide approval plans for books.[71] Such plans are often managed centrally, bringing in monographs on many subjects as, for example, with an approval plan for approval books. In some institutions, the plan provides for payment for approval books from a central fund, leaving the music materials budget to focus on printed music and recordings and such other books as are not be covered by the plan.

While book plans have been demonstrated to work well for libraries, approval plans for printed music and recordings can be more complicated, and opinions about their efficacy are mixed. At a roundtable discussion by conservatory librarians at the 2005 national meeting of the Music Library Association, one librarian reported a good experience with the library's score approval plan, while another school's was declared "a disaster." The report concluded that "because music is so idiosyncratic, libraries prefer to micromanage their collections. . . ."[72]

Writing an approval-plan profile for books can be relatively straightforward: after selecting subjects to be included (possibly according to relevant Library of Congress classifications), there are decisions to be made about particular publishers to be excluded and those to be covered comprehensively, preference for hardbound or paperbound if both are available, price limits, geographical coverage, and languages. Reprints and collections of previously published articles are typically excluded; books published in numbered series may also be excluded, or furnished selectively, based on a list of the library's existing standing orders.

In the case of printed music, there are many more decisions to make, in part because of the number of formats in which a work might be published, and other variables already discussed (bound versus unbound is rarely an issue, since most printed music is published only in paper covers). Approval plans for scores are commonly defined by publisher (for pre-twentieth-century repertory), or by composer (for twentieth- and twenty-first-century repertory).[73] For the former, the profile identifies a group of publishers for which comprehensive coverage is desirable; for the latter, the profile identifies a group of composers to be collected. Specialty publishers that focus on repertoire of particular interest to a significant number of the library's users would be appropriate choices for a publisher plan—Green Man Press and Garri Editions for practical performing editions of baroque vocal music, Robert Ostermeyer Musikedition for nineteenth-century music for horn, and Wayne Leupold Editions for organ music, to cite three examples. Subsets of a publisher's output can also be profiled, such as Bärenreiter Verlag's extracts for practical performance from its critical collected editions. For both publisher- and composer-type profiles, the plan should specify limiting factors, such as maximum cost for an individual edition; preferred formats for orchestral and dramatic music (conductor's score, study score, and/or vocal score); whether parts are to be furnished, if available, with chamber music scores; solo instruments that are to be excluded; whether to exclude choral octavo editions and music for children; and so forth.

Fortunately, vendors that service music approval plans—see the chapters on printed music and recordings for who they are—offer plenty of help. They have convenient checklists of formats and related issues for the selector to work through in developing a profile, as well as extensive lists of twentieth- and twenty-first-century composers from which to select names for inclusion on an approval-plan. For examples, see the Web site of Theodore Front Musical Literature, which services approval plans for North American and/or European score publications, as well as approval plans for recordings (http://www.tfront.com/info/approval_plan.php). Posted there are baseline lists of North American and European printed-music publishers and ongoing music series that are commonly included in its approval plans, and in May 2007, a list of 7,140 (!) contemporary composers—from Frank Abbinanti to Ginger Zyskowski—from which selectors can define an approval plan. There is also a worksheet and a preliminary order form.[74] Although some vendors rank contemporary composers from the well-known and prominent (rank 1), to the emerging and not yet widely performed or recorded (rank 3), it may not be a good idea to rely solely on vendors' rankings; asking for input from local faculty, particularly from composers, can be invaluable for fine-tuning a contemporary-composer list (as well as being a good public-relations move).

It is not unknown for a group of libraries to split up, say, the third-ranked composers on a vendor's list, each agreeing to purchase those in a portion of the alphabet, and to lend them freely to the other cooperating libraries. Such arrangements require long-term commitments, and they involve some risk, since some of the partners could find their collections lacking any works at all by a third-rank composer who is unexpectedly catapulted into the first rank.

Once the initial composer list is "set," it must be monitored and updated continually, as new names come to the fore. For this, the librarian needs to be aware of goings-on in the contemporary-music scene (see the section on "Keeping Current" in this chapter for some strategies for doing this). And those faculty composers who generously helped compile the original list should be encouraged to submit information about new composers and works of interest as they become aware of them.

It should not be necessary to emphasize that all aspects of a music approval plan—not just a contemporary-composers list—should be monitored. A profile, like a violin, must be tuned continually, and information should be shared and reviewed with the vendor when things go awry. The librarian who declared an approval plan to be a "disaster" might have been able, with heightened vigilance, to downgrade to something more along the line of "temporarily out of order."

# Associations and Societies

## PRIMARILY FOR LIBRARIANS AND ARCHIVISTS

### Music Library Association (MLA)

Music Library Association (MLA), http://www.musiclibraryassoc.org/. "Founded in 1931, MLA is the professional organization in the United States devoted to music librarianship and all aspects of music materials in libraries."[75] Resources on the Web site include a job placement service and list of available positions; descriptions of awards and grants given by the association; a guide to music copyright; career resources; and links to other resources, including the association's e-mail discussion list (MLA-L). Links to the eleven regional chapters of the association are at http://www .musiclibraryassoc.org/association/chapters.shtml.

PUBLICATIONS

MLA publications provide a broad spectrum of music and musicology resources.

> *Basic Manual Series*: "A comprehensive series of manuals designed to assist the librarian in dealing with various aspects of the organization, administration and use of a music library."

> *Index and Bibliography Series*: "A series of bibliographies, indexes, checklists, discographies and other types of guides to music and music literature. All areas of music study are covered, including popular music, American music, historical bibliography, new musicology, ethnomusicology and projects with potential to reach the broader musical public."

*Music Cataloging Bulletin*: "A monthly publication announcing internal policy and operational decisions and communications from the Library of Congress and reporting general cataloging news that may impact music cataloging."

*Newsletter*: Contains reports from MLA officers, committees, roundtables, regional chapters, and summaries of national conferences. Posted quarterly on the association's Web site.

*Notes: Quarterly Journal of the Music Library Association.* Contains scholarly articles on musicological and music library topics, and extended reviews of books, scores, sound recordings, video recordings, and digital media. Regular features include lists of books recently published (based on Library of Congress cataloging output), announcements of new catalogs from music publishers, new periodicals, and an annual summary of "Prices of Music Monographs and Scores as Reflected in *Notes*."[76]

*Technical Reports*: "Each volume in the series provides a focused, in-depth look at the practical side of the music library profession. Topics include cataloging, audio technology, and facilities management as well as reports of current research in music librarianship."

*MLA Membership Handbook*: Annual directory of the membership, including an outline of administrative structure with identities of office holders; lists of present and past presidents, *Notes* editors, award recipients, association contributors, patrons, and honorary members; list of MLA annual meetings.

## PUBLICATION AWARDS

The following awards are given annually.

*Vincent H. Duckles Award:* For the best book-length bibliography or other research tool in music.

*Richard S. Hill Award:* For the best article on music librarianship or article of a music-bibliographic nature.

*Eva Judd O'Meara Award:* For the best review published in *Notes*.

## OTHER MLA AWARDS AND HONORS

*Dena Epstein Award:* To support archival and library research in American Music.

*Carol June Bradley Award:* To support studies that involve the history of music libraries or special collections.

*Walter Gerboth Award:* In support of members who are in the first five years of their professional careers, to assist research-in-progress in music or music librarianship.

*Kevin Freeman Travel Grant:* To students, recent graduates, or other colleagues who are new to the profession for support to attend association annual meetings.

*MLA Citation:* To a librarian in recognition of a distinguished career. Citation recipients become honorary members of the association.

*MLA Special Achievement Award:* In recognition of an extraordinary service to the profession of music librarianship over a relatively short period of time.

## Music OCLC Users Group (MOUG)

Music OCLC Users Group (MOUG), http://www.musicoclcusers.org/. "The mission of the Music OCLC Users Group (MOUG) is to identify and provide an official means of communication and assistance for those users of the products and services of the Online Computer Library Center, Inc. (OCLC) concerned with music materials in any area of library service, in pursuit of quality music coverage in these products and services." On the group's Web site are links to cataloging tools and the NACO-Music Project Web site, an archive of issues of the newsletter, and information about the group's e-mail electronic discussion list. The group's annual conferences are usually scheduled in conjunction with the annual MLA conference, beginning the day before latter opens, at the same conference hotel.

### PUBLICATIONS

*Newsletter*: contains articles and reports on the group's activities. Regular features include "News from OCLC," "News from the Library of Congress," and music cataloging "Questions and Answers," with answers from the OCLC–MOUG liaison. Mailed three times per year to members. Back issues are archived at the Web site.

*The Best of MOUG*, 8th ed. (2008): "contains Library of Congress Name Authority File records for C. P. E. Bach, J. S. Bach, Beethoven,

Boccherini, Brahms, Clementi, Handel, Haydn, Mozart, Schubert, Schumann, Telemann and Vivaldi. There are also lists arranged by thematic number for Bach, Handel, Mozart, Schubert, Telemann and Vivaldi (F. and RV). It also contains English cross-references for Bartók, Dvořák, Glazunov, Gliere, Glinka, Grechaninov, Janáček, Kodály, Martinu, Mussorgsky, Prokofiev, Rachmaninoff, Rimsky-Korsakov, Shostakovich, Smetana, Stravinsky and Tchaikovsky. Each list includes uniform titles and corresponding authority record control numbers. Also includes book reviews

### AWARD

MOUG Distinguished Service Award: Honors "a librarian who has made significant professional contributions to music users of OCLC."

# International Association of Music Libraries, Archives, and Documentation Centres (IAML)

International Association of Music Libraries, Archives, and Documentation Centres (IAML), http://www.iaml.info/. "IAML encourages and promotes the activities of music libraries, archives and documentation centres to support and facilitate the realization of projects in music bibliography, music documentation and music library and information science at national and international levels." Resources on the Web site include: descriptions of the association's branches, commissions, and committees, reports from national branches, an online forum, and a link to the association's e-mail discussion list (IAML-L).

### PUBLICATIONS

*Fontes Artis Musicae*: "This journal is the principal medium of communication for the business of the Association and features articles relevant to the purposes of IAML, particularly in the area of music librarianship and documentation, bibliography and musicology. Also includes book reviews."

*IAML Electronic Newsletter*: Available online at http://www.iaml.info/en/newsletter.

## JOINT PROJECTS AND ASSISTED PUBLICATIONS

"Through joint commissions, IAML co-sponsors with other international associations, notably the IMS (International Musicological Society), four major bibliographical series for music scholars and librarians ('the four Rs'). These are all produced by cooperation between national groups and an international centre responsible for collecting and coordinating national contributions. The series may be ordered from their respective publishers." Find more information about these projects online at: http://www.iaml .info/activities/joint_projects.

*Répertoire international des sources musicales* (RISM): "International Inventory of Musical Sources is an international non-profit making organization with the objective of describing adequately the sources of music worldwide."

*Répertoire international de littérature musicale* (RILM): "International Inventory of Musical Literature is an ongoing abstracted bibliographic database of scholarly writings on music worldwide, available in annual print volumes, online (through OCLC and NISC), and on CD-ROM (through NISC). The International RILM Center is located at the City University of New York Graduate School and University Center."[77]

*Répertoire international d'iconographie musicale* (RIdIM): "International Inventory of Musical Iconography documents visual materials relating to music. RIdIM publishes catalogues, studies, a RIdIM/RCMI newsletter, the RIdIM/RCMI inventory of music iconography series, and sponsors a scholarly yearbook, Imago musicae (published by Duke University Press and Bärenreiter-Verlag). The RIdIM/RCMI (Research Center for Musical Iconography) is located at the City University of New York."

*Répertoire international de la presse musicale* (RIPM): "Retrospective Index to Music Periodicals (1800–1950) is the most recent of the four 'repertories.' Since 1987, it has produced approximately ten volumes per year offering access to a significant portion of the nineteenth- and early twentieth-century musical press. The Répertoire international de la presse musicale series is published in print, on the internet, and on CD-ROM by the National Information Services Corporation (NISC), and on the internet by EBSCO, NISC and OCLC. The editorial headquarters for RIPM (The RIPM International Center) is affiliated with the University of Maryland at College Park and is located in Baltimore, Maryland. In the summer of 2006 RIPM will celebrate the publication of its two hundredth volume, a database containing 500,000+ annotated records, and the birth of the RIPM Online Archive of Music Periodicals."[78]

## Association for Recorded Sound Collections (ARSC)

Association for Recorded Sound Collections (ARSC), http://www.arsc-audio.org/. "Founded in 1966, the Association for Recorded Sound Collections (ARSC) is a non-profit organization dedicated to research, study, publication, and information exchange surrounding all aspects of recordings and recorded sound. . . . The organization is comprehensive in scope and reflects the interests and concerns of its members, including: collectors, dealers, appraisers, archivists, librarians, historians, musicians, students, discographers, reviewers, media producers and recording engineers."

### PUBLICATIONS

> *ARSC Journal*: "a bi-annual, peer reviewed publication that serves to document the history of sound recording and includes original articles on many aspects of research and preservation: biography; cataloging; copyright law; current research; discography; technical aspects of sound restoration, etc. Selected ARSC conference papers are a regular feature. The journal also includes book, CD-ROM and sound recording reviews, and publishes a running bibliography of articles appearing in other specialist publications and of related interest."

> *ARSC Newsletter*: Conference programs and reports, news of digitization and preservation projects, and news of members and grants. Available as PDF files on the association's Web site.

> *ARSC Bulletin*: "published annually and includes information and reports concerning ARSC's governance and activities."

### AWARDS FOR EXCELLENCE IN RECORDED SOUND RESEARCH

"Awards are given to authors of books, articles or recording liner notes. . . . A maximum of two awards are presented annually in each category, for best history (H) and best discography (D). Awards are presented to both the authors and publishers of winning publications." Award categories are recorded blues, rhythm & blues, or soul music; classical music; country music; folk, ethnic or world music; rap or hip-hop music; rock music; jazz music; and record labels and general history.

## International Association of Sound and Audiovisual Archives (IASA)

**International Association of Sound and Audiovisual Archives (IASA),** http://www.iasa-web.org/. "The International Association of Sound and Audiovisual Archives (IASA) was established in 1969 in Amsterdam to function as a medium for international co-operation between archives that preserve recorded sound and audiovisual documents." On the Web site are guidelines and policy statements on copyright, legal deposit, national discography, and links to related organizations.

**PUBLICATIONS**

> *IASA Journal*: "The IASA Journal is published twice a year and is sent to all members at IASA." A selection of articles from the journal is published at the Web site.
>
> *Information Bulletin*: Available on the Web site.
>
> *The IASA Cataloguing Rules: A Manual for Description of Sound Recordings and Related Audiovisual Media*, ed. by Mary Miliano (1999).
>
> Standards, Recommended Practices, and Strategies: The Safeguarding of the Audio Heritage: Ethics, Principles and Preservation Strategy, ed. by Dietrich Schuller (2004).

# PRIMARILY FOR SCHOLARS AND EDUCATORS

Many music librarians are members and active participants in the organizations described below.

## American Musicological Society (AMS)

**American Musicological Society (AMS),** http://www.ams-net.org/. "The American Musicological Society was founded in 1934 to advance research in the various fields of music as a branch of learning and scholarship. 3,600 individuals and 1,200 institutional subscribers from over forty nations participate in the Society." Subscription information for the society's electronic discussion list is on the Web site.

## PUBLICATIONS

*Journal of the American Musicological Society*: scholarly research, published since 1948, issued three times a year.

*AMS Newsletter*: published semiannually in February and August. Issues are available at no charge on the society's Web site.

## PUBLICATION AWARDS

*Alfred Einstein Award:* For an outstanding article in musicology by a scholar in the early stages of professional work.

*Noah Greenberg Award:* For outstanding performance projects.

*Otto Kinkeldey Award:* For outstanding work of musicological scholarship (senior scholar).

*Lewis Lockwood Award:* For outstanding work of musicological scholarship (early stages).

*Claude V. Palisca Award:* For an outstanding edition or translation.

*H. Colin Slim Award:* For an outstanding article in musicology (senior scholar).

*Ruth A. Solie Award:* For an outstanding collection of essays.

*Robert M. Stevenson Award:* For outstanding scholarship in Iberian music.

*Philip Brett Award:* For outstanding work in gay, lesbian, bisexual, and transgender/transsexual studies (administered by the LBGTQ Study Group of the AMS).

## College Music Society (CMS)

College Music Society (CMS), http://www.music.org/cgi-bin/showpage .pl. "A consortium of college, conservatory, university, and independent musicians and scholars interested in all disciplines of music. Its mission is to promote music teaching and learning, musical creativity and expression, research and dialogue, and diversity and interdisciplinary interaction." Memberships are available only to individuals; there is no institutional membership category.

## PUBLICATIONS

*College Music Symposium*: "serves as a vehicle for the dissemination of information and ideas on music in higher education. The content of the publication highlights concerns of general interest and reflects the work of the Society in the areas of music represented on its Board of Directors. Issues of the publication focusing on specific topics may be developed if the need arises." Annual. Full text of current and past issues is available to members on the Web site.

*Newsletter*: Distributed five times a year to members.

*Directory of Music Faculties in Colleges and Universities, U.S. and Canada*: "Complete listings of institutions in higher education offering instruction in the fine and performing arts in the United States and Canada, including address, phone and fax numbers, and degree programs; Faculty listings for each institution including name, academic rank, highest degree earned, and teaching and research areas; Names and titles of administrators for each institution; Special section listing faculty by area of teaching interest; Complete listings of graduate degrees showing all schools where the degree is offered; Alphabetical faculty index; Alphabetical index of institutions; E-mail addresses." Annual. Available for subscription.

*CMS Sourcebooks in American Music*: Monographic series, distributed by Pendragon Press.

*Monographs and Bibliographies in American Music*: Monographic series, distributed by Pendragon Press.

*Music Vacancy List*: "the most comprehensive job listings available to musicians in higher education." Available online to members; monthly paper copy mailed for a small annual postage and handling fee.

## International Musicological Society (IMS)

International Musicological Society (IMS), http://www.ims-online.ch/news.aspx. "The International Musicological Society (IMS) was founded in 1927 in Basel, where it has its headquarters. It is a member of the Conseil International de la Philosophie et des Sciences Humaines (CIPSH), a branch organization of the UNESCO. Its purpose is the advancement of musicological research on the basis of international cooperation. Membership in IMS is open to all interested in musicological research, individuals as well as institutions, libraries and organisations." Links on the Web site are to national musicological societies (including AMS), and related international and national societies.

**PUBLICATIONS**

*Acta Musicologica*: Publishes research in multiple languages. Annual.

*Communiqués*: Annual news of the society, including its congresses.

## MENC: National Association for Music Education

MENC: National Association for Music Education (formerly Music Educators National Conference), http://www.menc.org/. "To advance music education by encouraging the study and making of music by all."

**PUBLICATIONS**

Print publications available to the public:

*Journal of Research in Music Education*: "Offers a collection of reports that includes thorough analyses of theories and projects by respected music researchers. Issued four times yearly."

*Music Educators Journal*: "Offers timely articles on teaching approaches and philosophies, current trends and issues in music education and the latest in products and services. Issued five times yearly."

*Teaching Music*: "Focuses on practical articles in specific areas. Includes guides on technology, advocacy resources and how-to articles in all specialty areas. Issued five times yearly."

Online publications for members only:

*General Music Today*: "Offers articles to keep you on top of emerging trends, effective lesson ideas, and new materials for teaching general music at all levels. Issued three times yearly."

*J.M.T.E.: Journal of Music Teacher Education:* "Focuses on topics of interest to professors involved in music teacher training. Brings you information on reform movements, state-mandated curricula, and more. Issued two times yearly."

*Update*: "Offers a wealth of practical applications for research findings in general music, choral, instrumental, and special topics in music education. Issued two times yearly."

Monographs: Titles are co-published with Rowman & Littlefield Education (http://www.rowmaneducation.com/).

## National Association of Schools of Music (NASM)

National Association of Schools of Music (NASM), http://nasm.arts-accredit.org/index.jsp?page=index. "NASM, founded in 1924, is an organization of schools, conservatories, colleges and universities. It has approximately 610 accredited institutional members. It establishes national standards for undergraduate and graduate degrees and other credentials. Institutional Membership is gained only through the peer review process of accreditation. Individual Membership is available by application. NASM has an extensive publications program." School re-accreditation occurs every ten years, and includes a self-study of the institution's music library collections.

## Society for American Music (SAM)

Society for American Music (SAM), http://american-music.org/. "The Society was founded in 1975 and was first named in honor of Oscar G.T. Sonneck, early Chief of the Music Division in the Library of Congress and pioneer scholar of American music. . . . The mission of The Society for American Music is to stimulate the appreciation, performance, creation and study of American music in all its diversity, and the full range of activities and institutions associated with that music. 'America' is understood to embrace North America, including Central America and the Caribbean, and aspects of its cultures everywhere in the world."

## PUBLICATIONS

*Journal of the Society for American Music*: Began publication as a quarterly in spring 2007. The society's previous official journal, *American Music*, continues as an independent publication from the University of Illinois Press.

*Society for American Music Bulletin*: Published three times a year; contains news, conference reports, and letters and short articles on appropriate topics.

## PUBLICATION AWARDS

*Irving Lowens Memorial Book Award*: Given annually "for the book judged as the best in the field of American music."

*Irving Lowens Memorial Article Award*: Given annually "for an article that, in the judgment of the awards committee, makes an outstanding contribution to the study of American music or music in America."

*Wiley Housewright Dissertation Award*: Annually, recognizes "a single dissertation on American music for its exceptional depth, clarity, significance, and overall contribution to the field. 'American' is understood here to embrace all of North America, including Central America and the Caribbean, and aspects of its cultures elsewhere in the world. Dissertations from American Studies, American history, and other fields beyond theory, musicology, and ethnomusicology are welcome as long as the primary focus of the work is a musical topic."

## Society for Ethnomusicology (SEM)

Society for Ethnomusicology (SEM), http://webdb.iu.edu/sem/scripts/home.cfm. "The Society for Ethnomusicology was founded in 1955 to promote the research, study, and performance of music in all historical periods and cultural contexts. At present, the Society for Ethnomusicology (SEM) has more than 2,500 members from six continents. The Society for Ethnomusicology is multidisciplinary in concept and worldwide in scope. Members' interests range from Japanese shakuhachi performance practice to popular musics in New York; from the conservation and display of Native

American musical instruments to teaching world music in public schools. Members of the Society for Ethnomusicology are scholars, students, performers, publishers, museum specialists, and librarians from numerous disciplines. Some of these disciplines include anthropology, musicology, cultural studies, acoustics, popular music studies, music education, folklore, composition, archiving, and the performing arts, just to name a few. . . . SEM members can access a special area of this website that contains position announcements, a searchable membership directory, downloadable newsletters, a calendar of SEM events and deadlines, and more."

## PUBLICATIONS

*Ethnomusicology*: "a refereed journal published three times each year by the University of Illinois Press. It features scholarly articles representing theoretical perspectives and research in ethnomusicology and related fields from an international perspective, as well as book, record, and film reviews. In addition, a current bibliography, discography, and film/videography ["ographies"] is published on this website in conjunction with each journal issue."

*SEM Newsletter*: Published four times each year; "contains valuable current information for ethnomusicologists: News of the annual meeting and a call for papers; a conference calendar; grant and fellowship announcements; and listing of professional opportunities in ethnomusicology and related disciplines. Members also contribute short articles and raise issues with the Society-at-large through published letters to the editor."

## PUBLICATION AWARDS

*Jaap Kunst Prize:* To recognize the most significant article in ethnomusicology written by a member of the society.

*Alan Merriam Prize:* To recognize the most distinguished English-language monograph in the field of ethnomusicology.

*Robert M. Stevenson Prize:* "To honor ethnomusicologists who are also composers by encouraging research, and recognizing a book, dissertation, monograph, edition, or paper (published or unpublished) on their compositional oeuvre. . . . This is not an award for the compositions themselves, but for research and publication on these compositions."

*Klaus P. Wachsmann Prize:* For advanced and critical essays in organology.

*Marcia Herndon Prize:* To honor exceptional ethnomusicological work in gender and sexuality including, but not limited to, works that focus on lesbian, gay, bisexual, two-spirited, homosexual, transgendered, and multiple-gender issues and communities (presented by the society's Gender and Sexualities Section).

## Society for Music Theory (SMT)

Society for Music Theory (SMT), http://www.societymusictheory.org/. "The Society for Music Theory was founded in 1977. The Society . . . encourages scholarly excellence by giving awards for outstanding publications in music theory. We also work to increase the diversity of our discipline and to promote fruitful exchanges between music theorists, musicologists, performers, and scholars in other fields." Information about the society's two electronic discussion lists (*SMT-announce*, and *SMT-talk*) is at http://www.societymusictheory.org/index.php?pid=63.

### PUBLICATIONS

*Music Theory Spectrum*: "the official print journal of the Society for Music Theory. It features articles on a range of topics in music theory and analysis, including aesthetics, history of theory, posttonal theory, critical theory, linear analysis, rhythm, and music cognition. Published twice a year, *Spectrum* features the best work in music theory, and is recognized as one of the foremost journals in the field."

*Music Theory Online (MTO)*: "an electronic journal that features peer-reviewed articles, book reviews, job announcements, a new books list, and a new dissertations list."

*SMT Newsletter*: "sent out to the membership in mid-February and August; an online version is also available. The Newsletter features important information on national and regional theory conferences, awards, calls for papers and articles, grant and fellowship information, and general news about people in the field."

**PUBLICATION AWARDS**

> *Wallace Berry Award:* For a distinguished book by an author of any age or career stage.
>
> *Outstanding Publication Award:* For a distinguished article by an author of any age or career stage.
>
> *Emerging Scholar Award:* For a book or article by an author in an early stage of her/his career.

# MISCELLANEOUS ORGANIZATIONS

The following U.S.-based specialist organizations are devoted to particular composers, instruments, genres, periods, and the like. Each produces one or more journals or newsletters that can be acquired for the library by institutional membership or by subscription. Some of these organizations also publish monographs.

Given here are names of organizations, titles of principal publications, and URLs where additional information can be found.

> American Bach Society, *Bach Notes*, http://www.americanbachsociety .org/
>
> American Brahms Society, *Newsletter*, http://brahms.unh.edu/
>
> American Choral Directors Association, *Choral Journal*, http://www .acdaonline.org/
>
> American College of Musicians / National Guild of Piano Teachers, *Piano Guild Notes*, http://pianoguild.com/
>
> American Composers Forum, *Sounding Board*, http://www .composersforum.org/
>
> American Guild of Organists, *The American Organist*, http://www .agohq.org/home.html
>
> American Handel Society, *Newsletter*, http://americanhandelsociety .org/
>
> American Harp Society, *American Harp Journal*, http://www.harp society.org/
>
> American Institute for Verdi Studies, *Verdi Forum*, http://www.nyu .edu/projects/verdi/

American Institute of Musicology, *Musica Disciplina*, http://www
.corpusmusicae.com/

American Liszt Society, *Journal of the American Liszt Society*, http://
www.americanlisztsociety.org/

American Music Therapy Association, *Journal of Music Therapy*,
http://www.musictherapy.org/

American Musical Instrument Society, *Journal of the American Musical Instrument Society*, http://www.amis.org/

American Orff-Schulwerk Association, *Orff Echo*, http://www.aosa2
.org/

American String Teachers Association, *American String Teacher*, http:
//www.astaweb.com/

American Viola Society, *Journal of the American Viola Society*, http://
www.americanviolasociety.org/

Boston Clavichord Society, *Tangents*, http://www.bostonclavichord
.org/

Center for Black Music Research, *Black Music Research Journal*, http://
www.cbmr.org/

Center for Schenkerian Studies, *Journal of Schenkerian Studies*, http://
web2.unt.edu/the/centers.php?css=css

Chamber Music America, *Chamber Music*, http://www.chamber
music.org/

Choristers Guild, *Chorister*, http://www.choristersguild.org/

Chorus America, *Voice of Chorus America*, http://www.chorusamerica
.org/

Church Music Association of America, *Sacred Music*, http://www
.musicasacra.com/

Early Music America, *Early Music America Magazine*, http://www
.earlymusic.org/

Film Music Society, *The Cue Sheet*, http://www.filmmusicsociety.org/

Guitar Foundation of America, *Soundboard*, http://www.guitar
foundation.org/

Historic Brass Society, *Historic Brass Society Journal*, http://www
.historicbrass.org/

Hymn Society in the United States and Canada, *The Hymn*, http://www.thehymnsociety.org/

International Alliance for Women in Music, *Women and Music*, http://www.iawm.org/

International Associated Schools of Jazz, *IASJ Newsletter*, http://www.iasj.com/

International Association for Jazz Education, *Jazz Education Journal*, http://www.iaje.org/

International Clarinet Association, *The Clarinet*, http://www.clarinet.org/home.asp

International Computer Music Association, *Conference Proceedings*, http://www.notam02.no/icma/

International Double Reed Society, *The Double Reed*, http://idrs2.colorado.edu/home/

International Horn Society, *The Horn Call*, http://www.hornsociety.org/

International Society of Bassists, *Bass World*, http://www.isbworldoffice.com/

International Trombone Association, *ITA Journal*, http://www.ita-web.org/

International Trumpet Guild, *ITG Journal*, http://www.trumpetguild.org/

International Tuba Euphonium Association, *ITEA Journal*, http://www.iteaonline.org/

Ira F. Brilliant Center for Beethoven Studies, *Beethoven Journal*, http://www.sjsu.edu/depts/beethoven/

Kurt Weill Foundation for Music, *Kurt Weill Newsletter*, http://www.kwf.org/

League of American Orchestras, *Symphony*, http://www.symphony.org/. Formerly American Symphony Orchestra League.

Lute Society of America, *Lute Society of America Quarterly*, http://www.cs.dartmouth.edu/~lsa/index.html

Major Orchestra Librarians' Association, *Marcato*, http://www.molainc.org/

Metropolitan Opera Guild, *Opera News*, http://www.metoperafamily
.org/guild/

Moravian Music Foundation, *Newsletter*, http://www.moravianmusic
.org/

Mozart Society of America, *Newsletter*, http://www.unlv.edu/mozart/

National Association for the Study and Performance of African American Music, *Con Brio*, http://naspaam.org/

National Association of College Wind and Percussion Instructors,
*NACWPI Journal*, http://www.nacwpi.org/

National Association of Pastoral Musicians, *The Liturgical Singer*,
http://www.npm.org/

National Association of Teachers of Singing, *Journal of Singing*, http://
www.nats.org/

National Flute Association, *Flutist Quarterly*, http://www.nfaonline
.org/

National Guild of Piano Teachers, *see* American College of Musicians

National Opera Association, *Opera Journal*, http://www.noa.org/

North American Saxophone Alliance, *Saxophone Symposium*, http://
www.saxalliance.org/

Opera America, *Opera America Newsline*, http://www.operaamerica
.org/

Organ Historical Society, *The Tracker*, http://www.organsociety.org/

Organization of American Kodály Educators, *Kodály Envoy*, http://
oake.org/

Percussive Arts Society, *Percussive Notes*, http://www.pas.org/

Performing Arts Medicine Association, *Medical Problems of Performing Artists Journal*, http://www.artsmed.org/

Polish Music Center, *Polish Music Journal*, http://www.usc.edu/dept/
polish_music/

Riemenschneider Bach Institute, *Bach Journal*, http://www.bw.edu/
academics/libraries/bach/

Sigma Alpha Iota International Music Fraternity for Women, *Pan
Pipes*, http://www.sai-national.org/

Society for Eighteenth Century Music, *Eighteenth-Century Music*, http://www.secm.org/

Society for Electro-Acoustic Music in the United States, *SEAMUS Journal*, http://www.seamusonline.org/

Society for Polish Music, *Musica Polonica*, http://www.polish-music .org/

Society for Seventeenth-Century Music, *Journal of Seventeenth-Century Music*, http://www.arts.uci.edu/sscm/

Society of Composers, Inc., *SCI Journal of Music Scores*, http://www .societyofcomposers.org/

Southeastern Historical Keyboard Society, *Early Keyboard Journal*, http://www.sehks.org/

Viola da Gamba Society of America, *Journal of the VdGSA*, http:// vdgsa.org/pgs/pubs.html

Violin Society of America, *Journal of the Violin Society of America*, http://www.vsa.to/

Westfield Center for Early Keyboard Studies, *Newsletter*, http://www .westfield.org/

# *Awards and Prizes*

K eeping up with awards, honors, prizes, and commissions in music can inform the selection of books, and printed and recorded music, through recognition of important work in scholarship, composition, and performance. Briefly described here are a few of the more prestigious and better-known programs. Music awards given in rotation with other arts categories are excluded, but several awards given simultaneously for music and other arts are included. Quoted descriptions are from the organizations' Web sites, where further information about award criteria, application procedures, lists of previous nominees and winners, and the like can be found.[79] Descriptions of awards presented by music societies and library organizations are found in the chapter on "Associations and Societies."

## COMPOSERS, COMPOSITIONS, AND COMMISSIONING PROGRAMS

**American Academy of Arts and Letters,** http://www.artsandletters.org/awards.php. Awards are by nomination, and, except for the Richard Rodgers awards, cannot be applied for. A panel of composer-members determines the winners of the following music awards.

*Academy Award:* "to encourage creative work in the arts. Now $7,500 each, Academy Awards are given annually: five to artists, eight to writers, four to composers, and three to architects."

*Marc Blitzstein Award:* "an award of $5,000 given periodically to a composer, lyricist, or librettist, to encourage the creation of works of merit for musical theater and opera."

*Walter Hinrichsen Award:* "given for the publication of a work by a mid-career American composer."

*Charles Ives Awards:* Endowed by the royalties of Charles Ives's works, for young composers. "Six scholarships of $7500 and two fellowships of $15,000 are now given annually. In 1998, the Academy inaugurated the Charles Ives Living [Award], which gives an American composer $75,000 a year for a period of three years. The purpose of this award is to free a promising talent from the need to devote his or her time to any employment other than music composition during the period of the award."

*Goddard Lieberson Fellowships:* Two fellowships of $15,000, "given annually to young composers of extraordinary gifts. The CBS Foundation endowed the fellowships in memory of the late president of CBS Records."

*Richard Rodgers Awards for Musical Theater:* "for the development of musical theater, [to] subsidize full productions, studio productions, and staged readings, by nonprofit theaters in New York City, of works by composers and writers who are not already established in this field."

Herb Alpert Award, http://www.alpertawards.org/. Established by the founder of the Tijuana Brass, who is also the "A" of A&M Records. "Inaugurated in 1994, the Alpert Award in the Arts provides annual fellowships of $50,000 to five artists, one each, in the fields of dance, film/video, music, theatre and the visual arts. Administered by California Institute of the Arts and funded by the Herb Alpert Foundation, the Awards support individuals working and living in the United States who have demonstrated exceptional talent and commitment to their craft, are generating an important body of work, and are likely to be recognized, within their discipline, as artists shaping a vital voice, vision or language. The Award honors artists whose work might be thought of as 'early mid-career' rather than well-established practitioners or those beginning their creative lives. In addition, it recognizes those artists particularly responsive to the complex, challenging and fertile role of the artist in society."

ASCAP Foundation Awards, http://www.ascapfoundation.org/awards.html. The American Society of Composers, Authors, and Publishers presents several annual awards to emerging composers and songwriters, and in recognition of the achievements of established composers and songwriters. ASCAP also presents student awards and scholarships too numerous to list here. Described below are awards that require submission of a score; not listed are ASCAP's awards for overall achievement.

*Young Jazz Composer Award: Sponsored by the Gibson Foundation,* "granted annually to encourage talented young jazz composers. Applicants must be citizens or permanent residents of the United States who have not reached their 30th birthday by December 31st."

*Morton Gould Young Composer Award:* "Open to composers in all musical genres . . . [to] encourage developing music creators during the earliest stages of their careers. This program selects several young composers recipients [sic] each year to receive the cash awards. . . . Each year the top award winner receives an additional cash prize, The ASCAP Foundation Leo Kaplan Award, named in memory of the distinguished jurist and music lover who served from 1967–1995 as ASCAP's Special Distribution Advisor."

*Rudolf Nissim Prize*: $5,000 is awarded annually for a work requiring a conductor (orchestra, band, or other large ensemble) that has not been performed professionally.

**Avery Fisher Prize.** Founded in 1974 by the philanthropist Avery Fisher, this prize is given to American musicians for outstanding achievement in classical music. The prize, at this writing worth $75,000, is administered by New York's Lincoln Center for the Performing Arts, and is not awarded every year. To date, all honorees have been instrumental concert and recording soloists, and ensembles.

**Fromm Music Foundation,** http://www.music.fas.harvard.edu/fromm.html. The foundation, created in 1952 by Illinois wine importer and philanthropist Paul Fromm, annually commissions the composition and performance of about 12 new works. Each composer is granted a commissioning fee of $10,000, and a subsidy is available to the ensemble performing the commissioned work. Since 1972, the program has been administered by Harvard University.

**Grawemeyer Award for Music Composition,** http://www.grawemeyer .org/. The award for 2008 is described as an "international prize in recognition of outstanding achievement by a living composer in a large musical genre: choral, orchestral, chamber, electronic, song-cycle, dance, opera, musical theater, extended solo work, etc. The award will be granted for a work premiered during the five-year period between 1 January 2002 and 31 December 2006."[80] The award was established in 1984 by H. Charles Grawemeyer—industrialist, entrepreneur, investor, philanthropist, and graduate of the University of Louisville in Kentucky, which administers the awards. Music composition was the first of the five Grawemeyer award categories (the others being Education, Improving World Order, Psychology, and Religion). The awards of $200,000 each make them among the most lucrative in their respective fields.

**John Simon Guggenheim Memorial Foundation Fellowships,** http://www .gf.org/index.html. The foundation "provides fellowships for advanced professionals in all fields (natural sciences, social sciences, humanities, creative arts) except the performing arts." Some 150 to 200 awards are given each year, and about seven to nine of them go to composers.

**Koussevitzky Music Foundations,** http://www.koussevitzky.org/. The joint commissioning programs of the Serge Koussevitzky Music Foundation in the Library of Congress, and the Koussevitzky Music Foundation, Inc. Koussevitzky commissions are awarded jointly to performing organizations, rather than directly to composers. "This commissioning program is designed primarily for orchestras and chamber groups that have a record of excellence in the performance of contemporary music. Commission fees for works for chamber groups range from $12,500 to $17,500. The Koussevitzky Foundations will fund the entire commission fee in the case of a work for a chamber group. The Foundations will fund up to $20,000 for a symphonic work, of which the submitting performing organization must provide at least 50% of the amount funded by the Foundations as a minimum matching grant." Composers' manuscripts for commissioned works are added to the collections of the Library of Congress.

**MacArthur Fellow Program,** http://www.macfound.org/. Presented by the John D. and Catherine T. MacArthur Foundation, and popularly known as the "MacArthur Genius Grants." The program "awards unrestricted fellowships to talented individuals who have shown extraordinary originality and dedication in their creative pursuits and a marked capacity for self-direction. There are three criteria for selection of Fellows: exceptional creativity, promise for important future advances based on a track record of significant accomplishment, and potential for the fellowship to facilitate subsequent creative work." The $500,000 grants are paid in quarterly installments over a five-year period. As of May 2008, thirty fellowships had been awarded to musicians.

**Paul Revere Awards** for outstanding printed-music design, http://www.mpa .org/paul_revere_awards/. Sponsored by the Music Publishers' Association of the United States, and named for Revolutionary War hero and silversmith Paul Revere, who was also America's first music engraver. A panel of judges annually assesses the clarity, creativity, and overall design of submitted publications in thirteen publishing categories. Copies of the winning editions are offered as a traveling exhibit, free to libraries on request, as scheduling allows. Photographs of award winners are displayed at the Web site.

**Pulitzer Prize in Music,** http://www.pulitzer.org/. One of several annual prizes in journalism, letters, and music, endowed by Joseph Pulitzer (1847–1911), publisher of the *New York World*, in a bequest to Columbia University. The music prize—first awarded in 1943—is for a work premiered in the United States between March 2 of the previous year and March 1 of the year of the award.

**William Schuman Award,** administered by Columbia University School of the Arts. The award, in the form of a direct, unrestricted grant of $50,000, is awarded in recognition of lifetime achievement. It was established in 1981 by a bequest from the family of composer William Schuman, and has been awarded irregularly.

# MUSIC RECORDINGS

## United States

In the United States, there are six major music awards—by which is understood recorded and film music—that provide excuses for putting on TV pageants. Three of these focus exclusively on popular-music genres, and two give awards for film music; the Grammys also honor excellence in classical-music recordings.

**Academy of Motion Picture Arts and Sciences Awards ("Oscars"),** http:// www.oscars.org/awardsdatabase/index.html. Annual awards include those for best movie song, and original score.

**American Music Awards.** Created in 1973 by showman Dick Clark to compete with the Grammys, these awards recognize artists, bands, and albums in the categories of pop/rock, soul/rhythm & blues, country, rap/hip-hop, adult contemporary, Latin, alternative, contemporary inspirational, and breakthrough new artist. Selection of winners is based on a poll of about 20,000 record buyers, so it is basically a popularity contest.

**Billboard Music Award,** http://www.billboard.com/. Like the American Music Awards, the Billboard Awards are based on popularity, as determined by *Billboard* magazine's year-end music charts. Presented annually in December since 1990, the awards recognize top-selling albums, singles, artists, songwriters, and producers in various pop categories; since 1992, a Billboard Century Award has also been presented to a classic pop artist (George Harrison was the first honoree).

**Golden Globe Awards,** http://www.goldenglobes.org/. Presented annually by the Hollywood Foreign Press Association, including awards for best motion picture song, and original score.

**Grammy Awards** (originally called the Gramophone Awards), http://www.grammy.com/. Sponsored by the National Academy of Recording Arts & Sciences, Inc. Academy members vote on five or six nominated recordings in each of 111 (in 2007) recording categories; the Grammys, therefore, are at least nominally about excellence rather than popularity. Pop-music awards are presented at a live, televised awards ceremony; classical and technical awards are announced off-camera, usually the preceding day.

**Rock and Roll Hall of Fame Induction Ceremony,** http://www.rockhall.com/hof/. Held annually in March and sponsored by the Rock and Roll Hall of Fame and Museum in Cleveland. Inductees are "the legendary performers, producers, songwriters, disc jockeys and others who have made rock and roll the force in our culture that it is." A small group of artists is honored each year for contributions to popular-music history. Eligibility is limited to artists and groups who released their first recordings at least twenty-five years before the award year. The ceremony is not aired live, but edited versions are usually shown later on VH1 cable.

## United Kingdom

*BBC Music Magazine* Awards, http://www.bbcmusicmagazine.com/. Annual awards for classical recordings, established in 2006. Readers cast votes for best of three jury-nominated recording in the categories of chamber music, orchestral, opera, vocal, choral, and instrumental music. In addition, the jury makes awards for the best newcomer, best premiere recording, technical excellence in recording, and two DVDs (one award each for a DVD performance and for a documentary).

Brit Awards, http://www.brits.co.uk/. Annual UK pop music awards founded (as the BPI Awards) in 1977 by the British Phonographic Industry, renamed in 1989 as the Britannia Awards, or Brit Awards. These are the British equivalent of the pop-music wing of the Grammy Awards, though the Brits are awarded in only fifteen categories. It is widely perceived that awards are based more on commercial success than artistic achievement.

Classic FM Gramophone Awards (before 2005, Gramophone Awards), http://www.gramophone.co.uk/voting.asp. Co-sponsored by the UK's *Gramophone* magazine and that nation's largest broadcaster of classical music. Winners are selected through a multistep process that begins with record companies' nominations, and concludes with votes by a *Gramophone* reviewing panel making six awards. Vote tallies for all finalists are published in the annual *Gramophone* Awards Issue.

Classical Brit Awards, http://classicalbrits.co.uk/. Established in 2000 as the classical-music equivalent of the Brit Awards and presented at an annual ceremony at the Royal Albert Hall in May—supporting young people in music and education. Proceeds from the event go to the British Record Industry Trust—BRIT, as luck would have it. Winners are chosen by an academy of music industry executives, the British Association of Record Dealers, members of the Musicians Union, and other industry insiders; the "Album of the Year" is voted its honor by listeners of Classic FM, the UK's first national, commercial radio station broadcasting classical music.

## Canada

Juno Awards, http://www.juno-awards.ca/. Presented to Canadian musicians and groups. Equivalent to the Grammys in the  United States.

The awards recognize all recorded musical categories, including popular, classical, world, and francophone. Winners are chosen by members of the Canadian Academy of Recording Arts and Sciences, or, depending upon the category, by a panel of experts, or actual record sales.

## France

**Grand Prix du Disque.** The principal French award for musical recordings. The award was begun by L'Académie Charles Cros in 1948, and offers prizes in various categories of classical, jazz, and world music. The categories vary from year to year, and multiple awards are often given in one category in the same year.

## International

**Cannes Classical Awards,** http://www.cannesclassicalawards.com/. Established by several international music magazines "to recognize the universal appeal of classical music in creating a truly international recording award, one in which the typical bias and local preferences common to these events are effectively counter-balanced by the multinational makeup of the jury." Several hundred critics from throughout Europe take part in a two-round voting process for nominees submitted by the recording industry in approximately twenty-eight different categories. Special awards such as those for lifetime achievement, artist of the year, and label of the year are selected by the chairman and the editors of the participating magazines. The award ceremony itself takes place in January at MIDEM (Marché international de l'édition musicale), the world's largest music industry trade fair, held annually in Cannes, France. Winners are announced by the participating journals in their first issues published after the ceremony. Also known as the MIDEM Classical Awards.

# *Getting Help*

This miscellany of online and print resources includes those that the present author consults regularly, or has had occasion to recommend to others, though they do not fall naturally within the topics discussed in previous chapters.

## MUSIC REFERENCE, SELECTION, AND ACQUISITION RESOURCES

### Doctoral Dissertations in Musicology–Online (DDM–Online)

http://www.chmtl.indiana.edu/ddm/. A browsable and fully searchable "international database of bibliographic records for completed dissertations and new dissertation topics in the fields of musicology, music theory, and ethnomusicology, as well as in related musical, scientific, and humanistic disciplines." Hosted by the Center for the History of Music Theory and Literature at Indiana University. Contains more than 13,700 records.

### International Association of Music Information Centres

http://www.iamic.net/. Links to the Web sites and catalogs of "43 member organisations in 38 countries. Music Information Centres across the world bear fundamental similarities: they provide specialised music resources for music students, performers, composers and music teachers; they act as visitor centres for any member of the public with an interest in learning about national musical heritage; they develop audiences for new music through educational and promotional projects." Some of these centers publish scores and recordings by composers of the nation.

## Internet Music Collection and Acquisition Resources

http://www.libraries.iub.edu/index.php?pageId=3897, compiled by R. Michael Fling for Indiana University's Cook Music Library, with links to book, score, and recording dealers and databases; out-of-print and antiquarian music resources; and directories of publishers, people, libraries, consortia, music information centers, and other online music sources.

## Music Selection Resources on the WWW

http://dslweb.nwnexus.com/aseaberg/, compiled by Anna Seaberg for the King County (Washington State) Library System, provides links to verification sources; popular-song indexes, and collections of images and lyrics; CD reviews; libraries; and a variety of music and music-librarianship resources.

## National Library Catalogs Worldwide

http://www.library.uq.edu.au/natlibs/. Links to national libraries and their catalogs in 99 countries. Hosted by the University of Queensland, Australia.

# USING THE ONLINE MUSIC CATALOG

## ALA-LC Romanization Tables

http://www.loc.gov/catdir/cpso/roman.html: To verify authorized transliteration patterns of names and titles in non-Roman alphabets such as Cyrillic, which is used in Russian book and score editions.

## Library of Congress Authorities

http://authorities.loc.gov/. To verify LC-authorized names, titles, and
subjects.

## Making the Most of the Music Library:
## Using Uniform Titles

http://library.music.indiana.edu/collections/uniform/uniform.html.
This interactive tutorial, created at Indiana University's Cook Music
Library, introduces users to the concept and structure of music uniform titles, which collate multiple editions and versions of a work in a
library's catalog. The music uniform title has been called the "master
achievement of music librarianship,"[81] and every person who searches
for musical works in a library's catalog—including patrons—must be
familiar with how these titles are structured in order to do so with
consistent success.

## The Music OCLC Users Group Presents
## the Best of MOUG

*A List of Library of Congress Name Authority Records for Music Titles of
Major Composers.* 8th ed., compiled by Margaret Kaus. Manhattan,
KS: MOUG, 2008. A *vade mecum* of authorized titles for many of the
works by 13 major composers, and title cross-references for the works
of 17 Slavic composers. Available from the editor. A printable order
form is on MOUG's Web site (http://www.musicoclcusers.org/bestof
mougorder.pdf).

## Types of Compositions for Use
## in Music Uniform Titles

http://www.library.yale.edu/cataloging/music/types.htm, compiled by
the MLA Working Group on Types of Compositions. Some musical works have distinctive titles (for example, *Cabaret, Symphonie*

*fantastique*), but many others use generic titles based on a type of composition such as a musical form (Sonata, Concerto), tempo designation (Adagio, Largo), or standard combination of instruments (String Quartet, Piano Trio). Other titles are difficult to categorize as distinctive or generic. This list is a reference for terms that the working group has designated as generic (and therefore requiring qualification by medium, number, or key signature in uniform titles) or distinctive (not requiring qualification).

## TERMS AND ABBREVIATIONS

Printed music and recordings are distributed from Bookland's back of beyond, where a regional dialect is written and spoken: terms and abbreviations often differ from those commonly used by mainstream book and journal publishers and vendors. Furthermore, the international nature of the music publishing and recording industries means that many of these terms and phrases are in foreign languages.

The following glossaries can be helpful to the selector in interpreting the language.

Boorman, Stanley. "Glossary," in *Music Printing and Publishing*, ed. by D. W. Krummel and Stanley Sadie, 489–550. Norton/Grove Handbooks of Music. New York: W. W. Norton, 1990.

Fling, R. Michael. "Glossary," in *Library Acquisition of Music*, 179–96. Music Library Association Basic Manual Series, 4. Lanham, MD: Scarecrow, for the Music Library Association, 2004.

Hixon, Donald L. *Music Abbreviations: A Reverse Dictionary*. Lanham, MD: Scarecrow, 2005.

Leach, Joel. *A Concise Guide to Music Industry Terms*. Pacific, MO: Mel Bay Publications, 2005.

Maple, Amanda and Jean Morrow. "Glossary," in *Guide to Writing Collection Development Policies for Music*, 93–97. Music Library Association Technical Reports, 26. Lanham, MD: Scarecrow, for the Music Library Association, 2001.

Thorin, Suzanne E. and Carole Franklin Vidali. *The Acquisition and Cataloging of Music and Sound Recordings: A Glossary*. MLA

Technical Reports, 11. Canton, MA: Music Library Association, 1984.[82]

## HELP BY E-MAIL

The best help can come from librarians who may have dealt with the same issue facing you now. MLA-L (http://www.musiclibraryassoc.org/resources/mla-l.shtml) is the Music Library Association's e-mail distribution list. In addition to serving as a channel for dissemination of information about the association's activities, MLA-L is intended also as an avenue for reference and other queries posted by individual subscribers. It is an invaluable resource whenever one has reached an apparent dead end trying to resolve a problem about any aspect of music collection development or other music library work. Every librarian who works with music should become a subscriber. Queries back to 1990 are archived, and searchable at http://listserv.indiana.edu/archives/mla-l.html.

# REFERENCE NOTES

1. The *Oxford English Dictionary*, 2nd ed. (OED Online, http://dictionary.oed.com/), gives fourteen main definitions for "Music" as a noun or adjective (excluding combination forms), and three as a verb. I leave it to others to comb for variant meanings in etymological dictionaries of other languages.

2. http://www.musiclibraryassoc.org/employmentanded/musiclibrarianship.shtml.

3. Michael Gorman, "Music Librarians," *Our Own Selves: More Meditations for Librarians* (Chicago: ALA, 2005), 219. For an earlier, but no less relevant discussion of what makes music libraries and librarians different from others, see Rita Benton, "The Nature of Music and Some Implications for the University Music Library," *Fontes Artis Musicae* 23, no. 1 (1976): 53–60.

4. Several authors in the last quarter century have plowed some of the same ground as the present guide, which has been informed by their writings. Among these are (in reverse chronological order): Daniel Zager, "Essential Partners in Collection Development: Vendors and Music Librarians," *Notes* 63, no. 3 (Mar. 2007): 565–73; R. Michael Fling, *Library Acquisition of Music: A Basic Manual,* Music Library Association Basic Manual Series, 4 (Lanham, Md.: Scarecrow, for the Music Library Association, 2004); Stephen Luttmann, "Selection of Music Materials," in *Selecting Materials for Library Collections,* ed. Audrey Fenner, 11–25, The Acquisitions Librarian, 31/32 (New York: Haworth, 2004); Zager, "Collection Development and Management," *Notes* 56, no. 3 (Mar. 2000): 567–73, which is one of thirteen articles in this issue of *Notes* that make up a symposium titled "Music Librarianship at the Turn of the Century," and which was published also that year as a monograph in the series Music Library Association Technical Reports, 27, ed. by Richard Griscom (Lanham, Md.: Scarecrow, 2000); Elisabeth Rebman, "Music," in *Humanities in the Library,* 2nd ed., ed. by Nancy Allen, 132–72 (Chicago: ALA, 1993); Nancy Bren Nuzzo, "Music Scores," in *Nonbook Media: Collection Management and User Services,* ed. by John W. Ellison and Patricia Ann Coty, 181–92 (Chicago: ALA, 1987); and Michael A. Keller, "Music," in *Selection of Library Materials in the Humanities, Social Sciences, and Sciences,* ed. Patricia A. McClung, 139–62 (Chicago: ALA, 1985). The older among these presentations have, naturally, become less relevant with the passage of time. For a comprehensive bibliography about collection development and management

of music, see Carol June Bradley, *American Music Librarianship: A Research and Information Guide,* Routledge Music Bibliographies (New York: Routledge, 2005), 1–53. The section lists 190 general books and articles on the topic, plus 229 bibliographies and 136 discographies related to music collection development published through the year 2000.

5. These variables make it nearly impossible to generalize about music collections in U.S. public libraries. Two surveys from the beginning of this century form the basis of comments in this paragraph: Linda B. Fairtile and Karen M. Burke, "Music Collections in American Public Libraries," *Fontes Artis Musicae* 48, no. 4 (Oct.–Dec. 2001): 327–41; and New England Chapter of MLA, Public Libraries Committee, "Music Collection and Acquisition Practices in Public Libraries in Connecticut," *MLA Newsletter* 120 (Mar.–Apr. 2000): 25–28.

6. Quoted by Richard Macnutt, "Early Acquisitions for the Paris Conservatoire Library: Rodolphe Kreutzer's Role in Obtaining Materials from Italy, 1796–1802," in *Music Publishing & Collecting: Essays in Honor of Donald W. Krummel,* ed. by David Hunter, 167–88 (Urbana: Graduate School of Library and Information Science, University of Illinois at Urbana-Champaign, 1994).

7. *Statuten der Gesellschaft der Musikfreunde des österreichischen Kaiserstaates* (Vienna: Anton Strauss, 1814), 4. My translation.

8. Victoria L. Cooper, *The House of Novello: Practice and Policy of a Victorian Music Publisher, 1829–1866,* Music in Nineteenth-Century Britain (Aldershot, Hants, Eng.; Burlington, Vt.: Ashgate, 2003), 30.

9. Malcolm Turner and Arthur Searle, "The Music Collections of the British Library Reference Division," *Notes* 38, no. 3 (Mar. 1982): 500.

10. Carol June Bradley, the doyenne of American music-library history, has documented these developments in several publications: "The Music Library Association: The Founding Generation and Its Work," *Notes* 37, no. 4 (June 1981): 763–822; *Music Collections in American Libraries: A Chronology,* Detroit Studies in Music Bibliography, 46 (Detroit: Information Coordinators, 1981); *American Music Librarianship: A Biographical and Historical Survey* (New York: Greenwood, 1990); and *American Music Librarianship: A Research and Information Guide,* Routledge Music Bibliographies (New York: Routledge, 2005), which is a classified bibliography of writings through the year 2000. See also Rita Benton, "An Introduction to American Music Libraries," *Fontes Artis Musicae* 9, no. 1 (1962): 28–33; June Rose Morroni, "The Music Library Association, 1931–1961" (M.A. thesis, University of Chicago, 1968); James Coover, "American Music Librarianship: The Formative Years and the First Generation," *Fontes Artis Musicae* 17, no. 3 (1970): 109–19; and Marjorie Hassen, "The Early Development of American Music Libraries Serving Academic Departments of Music," *Fontes Artis Musicae* 48, no. 4 (Oct.–Dec. 2001): 342–52.

11. A catalog of the books sold by Jefferson in 1815 is *Thomas Jefferson's Library: A Catalog with the Entries in His Own Order,* ed. by James Gilreath and Douglas L. Wilson (Washington, D.C.: Library of Congress, 1989). A transcription of the music

section of Jefferson's 1783 manuscript catalog of his library (reproduced in facsimile at http://www.thomasjeffersonpapers.org/catalog1783/), including printed editions and manuscript copies used for home music-making, is printed in Helen Cripe, *Thomas Jefferson and Music* (Charlottesville: University Press of Virginia, 1974), 97–104.

12. Sonneck also compiled the first subject-headings list for music: *A Provisional List of Subject Headings for Music: Based on the Library of Congress Classification* (Rochester, N.Y.: Sibley Musical Library, Eastman School of Music, 1933).

13. Music Teachers' National Association, *Music Departments of Libraries*, Bulletin of the Bureau of Education, U.S. Department of the Interior, 33 (Washington, D.C.: Govt. Printing Office, 1922).

14. Oscar Sonneck, "The History of Music in America: A Few Suggestions," in *Studies in Musical Education History and Aesthetics*, Papers and Proceedings of the Music Teachers' National Association, 38th annual meeting, 1916 (Hartford, Conn.: the Association, 1917), 54.

15. Published in December 1932 as vol. 19 of the *American Council of Learned Societies Bulletin.* Library information is on pp. 52–68.

16. These beginnings are recounted in considerable detail by Morroni, "The Music Library Association"; and by Bradley, "The Founding Generation."

17. From around 1700, and well into the 20th century, music typically was printed without dates of publication. "With the development of a music publishing industry after 1700, which produced copies from engraved plates rather than from movable type . . , the plates could be stored easily, and copies could be made at any time, [thus] the statement of a date became, in a sense, inappropriate": International Association of Music Libraries, Commission for Bibliographical Research, *Guide for Dating Early Published Music: A Manual of Bibliographical Practices*, comp. by D. W. Krummel (Hackensack, N.J.: Joseph Boonin; Kassel: Bärenreiter, 1974), 24. Absence of dates could also influence marketing, in accordance with Miss Hardcastle's observation in Oliver Goldsmith's *She Stoops to Conquer* (1773, act 3) that "Women and music should never be dated"; an edition reissued from old, undated plates could be passed off as music of the newest fashion.

18. George Sherman Dickinson, "Apologia for the MLA," *Notes* (1st ser.) 6 (Nov. 1938): 36–37.

19. For an extended, documented history of music study and scholarship, see Bernarr Rainbow, *Music in Educational Thought and Practice: A Survey from 800 BC*, reprint of 1989 ed., with new chapters by Gordon Cox (Woodbridge, Suffolk, Eng.; Rochester, N.Y.: Boydell Press, 2006). About music education in the United States, see Michael L. Mark and Charles L. Gary, *A History of American Music Education*, 3rd ed. (Lanham, Md.: Rowman & Littlefield Education, in partnership with MENC, the National Association for Music Education, 2007).

20. A bibliography of Sonneck's writings, with reprints of selections from them, is in *Oscar Sonneck and American music*, ed. by William Lichtenwanger (Urbana: University of Illinois Press, 1983).

21. Sonneck, "The History of Music in America: A Few Suggestions," 54.

22. Missoula, Mont.: College Music Society, 2006. For introductory essays on music collections serving two of these types of institutions, see Marjorie Hassen, "The Early Development of American Music Libraries Serving Academic Departments of Music," and Deborah Campana, "Music Libraries Supporting Comprehensive Schools of Music," *Fontes Artis Musicae* 48, no. 4 (Oct.–Dec. 2001): 342–52, and 353–61, respectively.

23. For overviews of music printing and publishing, see H. Edmund Poole and Richard Vendome, "Music Printing"; and D. W. Krummel, "Music Publishing"; in *Music Printing and Publishing*, ed. D. W. Krummel and Stanley Sadie, 3–78 and 79–132, respectively, Norton/Grove Handbooks in Music (New York: W. W. Norton, 1990). See also Stanley Boorman, Eleanor Selfridge-Field, and D. W. Krummel, "Printing and Publishing of Music," in Grove Music Online, http://www.grovemusic.com (the Krummel section on "Publishing," at II, is a reprint with minor revisions of his chapter in the Norton/Grove Handbook publication cited immediately above).

24. A score is "A visual representation of a musical work, usually printed or written, in which all of the two or more parts of an ensemble that are supposed to be heard simultaneously are aligned vertically, each part on a separate staff. . . . In casual use, all music editions are sometimes referred to as scores, as distinguished from writings about music, and recordings." A part is "The music for any one voice or instrument that contributes to the texture of a musical work. (2) The visual representation, commonly printed or written of (usually) one such part for use by (usually) one performer." From the glossary in Fling, *Library Acquisition of Music*, 193 and 190, respectively.

25. James Grier, "Editing," Grove Music Online, http://www.grovemusic.com/, at 6, "Types of Edition." A more expansive discussion of this topic is Grier's *The Critical Editing of Music: History, Method, and Practice* (Cambridge; New York: Cambridge University Press, 1996).

26. A dealer specializing in music facsimiles is OMI: Old Manuscripts & Incunabula, http://www.omifacsimiles.com/. Until recently, OMI mailed catalogs and lists of recent facsimile publications to its customers; today, clients must take the initiative to visit the Web site, where PDF catalogs list more than 8,000 available music facsimiles, with bibliographic citations and annotations.

27. Music manuscripts and early printed editions that have *not* been published commercially in facsimile can often be acquired as microfilm or photographic reproductions directly from the libraries that own the originals, or from special microfilm archives like the Deutsches Musikgeschichtliches Archiv (http://www.dmga.de/) in Kassel, Germany, which since 1954 has been documenting on microfilm the music composed 1450–1800 by German composers, and by foreign composers whose works have been found in sources of German provenance. A partial contents listing is on the Web site. On the founding and purpose of the DMA, see Harald Heckmann, "Archive of German Music History," *Notes* 16, no. 1 (1958): 35–42. Concerning some of the problems encountered in acquiring microfilm sources directly from libraries and archives, see Fling, *Library Acquisition of Music,* 149–59.

28. Quoted from a description of the project in "Notes for *Notes*," *Notes* 64, no. 3 (Mar. 2008): 475–76. Access to the images will be through the library's online public catalog, CORSAIR (http://corsair.themorgan.org/).

29. Similar, if not truly analogous, are guitar editions in today's popular-music realm; along with traditional notation are printed "frames" or "tab notation"—graphic representations of the instrument's fretboard, showing with symbols or numbers where the fingers are to be placed upon it.

30. *Harvard Dictionary of Music*, 4th ed., ed. by Don Michael Randel (Cambridge, Mass.: Belknap Press of Harvard University Press, 2003), s.v. "Editions, historical," by Harold E. Samuel, rev. Lenore Coral.

31. Fallen Leaf Reference Books in Music, 14 (Berkeley, CA: Fallen Leaf Press, 1997).

32. 2 vols. (Chicago: ALA, 1980).

33. Published by the National Information Services Corp. (NISC) of Baltimore, Md. A fact sheet with additional information about this database is at the NISC Web site, http://www.nisc.com/factsheets/images/qghi.pdf. Obligatory full disclosure: I am a content editor for this online resource, meaning that I review index entries for musicological correctness, and conformity to the project's specifications for entries.

34. Hartmut Walravens, "The International Standard Music Number (ISMN): A History and Current Status Report," *Fontes Artic Musicae* 54, no.2 (Apr.–Jun. 2007): 204–207.

35. See the Web site of the International ISMN Agency, http://www.ismn-international.org/.

36. A bibliography of some additional national bibliographies that list printed music is found in Fling, *Library Acquisition of Music*, 205–208.

37. http://www.emusicquest.com/. Emusicquest is the online successor to the venerable Music-in-Print Series for various instrumental and vocal media that were published by Musicdata, 1974–99. Many of the original volumes are still in print (though outdated), or have been issued on CD-ROM; availability and prices of these are listed at the Emusicquest Web site.

38. "Sheet music" has two meanings: "(1) Unbound songs, piano pieces, etc., of up to eight pages of printed music, the usual printed format for popular songs up until the late twentieth century. (2) Sometimes used imprecisely to refer to any kind of printed music, as distinguished from recorded music"—from the glossary in Fling, *Library Acquisition of Music*, 193. *Books in Print*'s usage is, in context, clearly (2).

39. Michael A. Keller, "Music," in *Selection of Library Materials in the Humanities, Social Sciences, and Sciences*, ed by Patricia A. McClurg, 139–62, at 142 (Chicago: ALA, 1985).

40. Advisory editor, Michael A. Keller (New York: Schirmer Books, 1997), 257–97.

41. Elizabeth Davis, coordinating editor; Pamela Bristah and Jane Gottlieb, scores editors (Chicago: ALA, 1997). Obligatory full disclosure: I was involved editorially in the 2nd edition, which had a different focus: *A Basic Music Library: Essential Scores and Books* (Chicago: ALA, 1983). At this writing, a fourth edition is in preparation, though its focus and format have not been announced.

42. For a concise history of sound recording, see Arthur Ord-Hume, Jerome F. Weber, and John Borwick, "Recorded Sound," Grove Music Online (2001), http://www .grovemusic.com, at I: "History of Recording." For a more extended history, to about 1990, see Pekka Gronow and Ilpo Saunio, *An International History of the Recording Industry*, trans. from the Finnish by Christopher Moseley (New York: Cassell, 1998).

43. Donna Mendell, et al., "The Role of Reviewing Media in the Selection of Classical Recordings," *Collection Management* 18, nos. 1–2 (1993): 71–88.

44. For more about these and other recordings awards, see the chapter on "Awards and Prizes."

45. In a *New York Times* review of 29 January 2006, Allan Kozinn remarked that "Classical musicians generally avoided naming their recordings until recently. . . . With few exceptions, classical disc titles seem either silly or confusing, and unlikely to stand the test of time." Kozinn may have a point, in that he was reviewing an Oxingale Records CD titled *Mozart the Mason*, which he noted contained none of Mozart's Masonic music.

46. Virgil Blake, "Picking the Hits: The Reviewing of Popular Music Recordings," *Collection Management* 11, no. 3–4 (1989): 23–58.

47. David Laing, "Chart," Grove Music Online (2001), http://www.grovemusic.com/. For further information about charts, see Paul Allen, "Charts, Airplay and Promotion," chapter 8 in *Record Label Marketing*, by Thomas W. Hutchison, Amy Macy, and Paul Allen, 143–61 (Boston: Focal Press, 2006).

48. For an overview of the publishing of music books in the U.S., see Michael Ochs, "What Music Scholars Should Know about Publishers," *Notes* 59, no. 2 (Dec. 2002): 288–300.

49. New York: R. R. Bowker, 1960–.

50. For a full list of CIP exclusions, see http://cip.loc.gov/scope.html.

51. Introduction to the 2006 installment, 53, no. 4 (Oct.–Dec. 2006): 362–468.

52. For more information on this service, see http://www.loc.gov/cds/mds.html.

53. Older bibliographies of music monographic series, now hopelessly outdated or of limited scope, are Fred Blum, *Music Monographs in Series: A Bibliography of Numbered Monograph Series in the Field of Music Current since 1945* (New York: Scarecrow Press, 1964); Sydney Robinson Charles, *A Handbook of Music and Music Literature in Sets and Series* (New York: Free Press, 1972); and Hermann Walther, *Bibliographie der Musikbuchreihen: 1886–1990*, Catalogus musicus, 12 (Kassel: Bärenreiter, 1991). The first two of these are international in scope; the third lists only titles published in German-language countries.

54. Obligatory full disclosure: I am an assistant editor of this journal. My primary responsibility is to copy-edit all of the articles, and all of the reviews of printed music.

55. For fuller discussion of the publishing process, see the Michael Ochs article cited in n. 47.

56. Links to the online catalogs of these and many other university presses, including those that publish fewer music titles, or titles primarily of regional interest, are found in the Web directory of membership of the Association of American University Presses, http://aaupnet.org/membership/directory.html.

57. *Notes* 64, no. 2 (Dec. 2007): 249.

58. According to the geographical-chronological listing in Imogen Fellinger, et al., "Periodicals" (rev. 29 July 2003), Grove Music Online, http://www.grovemusic.com.

59. "Identifying Uniform Core Journal Titles for Music Libraries: A Dissertation Citation Study," *College & Research Libraries* 60, no. 2 (Mar. 1999): 153–63.

60. From the column's headnote in vol. 63, no. 1 (Sept. 2006).

61. From the JSTOR Web site, http://www.jstor.org/about/desc.html: "JSTOR is a not-for-profit organization with a dual mission to create and maintain a trusted archive of important scholarly journals, and to provide access to these journals as widely as possible. JSTOR offers researchers the ability to retrieve high-resolution, scanned images of journal issues and pages as they were originally designed, printed, and illustrated. . . . JSTOR is not a current issues database. Because of JSTOR's archival mission, there is a gap, typically from one to five years, between the most recently published journal issue and the back issues available in JSTOR." A list by discipline of journals archived in JSTOR (fifty-six music titles as of May 2008) is available on the Web site.

62. Of secondary importance for music are Arts and Humanities Citation Index: AHCI (http://scientific.thomson.com/products/ahci/) and International Index to the Performing Arts: IIPA (http://iipa.chadwyck.com/marketing.do). Readers are directed to the Web sites of these services for information about them.

63. Leslie Troutman, "Comprehensiveness of Indexing in Three Music Periodical Index Databases"; and Alan Green, "Keeping Up with the Times: Evaluating Currency of Indexing, Language Coverage and Subject Area Coverage in the Three Music Periodical Index Databases"; *Music Reference Services Quarterly* 8, no. 1 (2001): 39–51, and 53–68, respectively. A comparison of the modes of access to RILM Abstracts data as provided by five database vendors, written by Donna Arnold, Judy Clarence, Stephen Luttmann, and Holling Smith-Borne, was published in *Notes* 61, no. 1 (Sept. 2004): 197–205.

64. Green, "Keeping Up," 66.

65. Review by Paul Cary is in *Notes* 64, no. 3 (Mar. 2008): 555–63.

66. A review by Diana R. Hallman of the online version is in *Notes* 58, no. 2 (Dec. 2001): 408–11.

67. *Bowker Annual of Library and Book Trade Information* 51 (2006): 497.

68. For earlier collection policy recommendations for music, see Edward Lein, "Suggestions for Formulating Collection Development Policy Statements for Music Score Collections in Academic Libraries," *Collection Management* 9 (1987): 69–89.

69. Adapted from the eleven "canons" promulgated by Donald W. Krummel in "Observations on Library Acquisitions of Music," *Notes* 23, no. 1 (Sept. 1966): 13–14.

70. The literature on approval plans is extensive, though little has been written about approval plans specifically for music. See, however, Daniel Zager's discussion in "Essential Partners in Collection Development: Vendors and Music Librarians," *Notes* 63, no. 3 (Mar. 2007): 565–75, esp. 569–73; the present discussion is based in part upon Zager's. Among some recent general guides to approval plans, and the principles that inform them, are *Approval Plans: Issues and Innovations*, ed. by John H. Sandy, Acquisitions Librarian Series, 16 (New York: Haworth, 1996); *Guide to Managing Approval Plans*, ed. by Susan Flood, Acquisition Guidelines, 11 (Chicago: ALA, Association for Library Collections & Technical Services, 1998); and *Evolution & Status of Approval Plans*, comp. by Susan Flood, SPEC Kits, 221 (Washington, D.C.: Association of Research Libraries, Office of Management Services, 1997). The last-named of these titles contains results of a survey of ARL libraries conducted in the mid-1990s, with documentation about approval plans from six of the seventy-five responding libraries, and a brief bibliography.

71. Approval plans are used primarily for acquiring traditional print materials (books), according to *Evolution & Status of Approval Plans*, though 30 percent of respondents to that survey indicated using such plans as a way of acquiring nonprint media. The number of libraries using approval plans to acquire printed music and sound recordings was not addressed by the survey.

72. "Conservatory Libraries Roundtable," reported by Richard Vallone, *MLA Newsletter* 141 (May–June 2005): 118. At the 2008 meeting of MLA's Small Academic Libraries Roundtable, a show of hands demonstrated that "very few" institutions in that category with representatives in attendance were using approval plans. Reported by Barbara A. Walzer, *MLA Newsletter,* 152 (Mar.–Apr. 2008): 14.

73. This dual composer–publisher construct for music approval plans is advocated by Zager, "Essential Partners," 570.

74. Otto Harrassowitz (http://www.harrassowitz.de/) services approval plans for European score editions, and for music books from German-language areas. J. W. Pepper (http://www.jwpepper.com/blanket_order.pdf) services approval plans for North American score editions. Composer lists and other specific details about their plans are not posted online.

75. Quoted text in this section is from the organizations' Web sites.

76. Obligatory full disclosure: I am an assistant editor of this journal, for which I copy-edit all of the articles and music reviews.

77. About RILM, see Barbara Dobbs Mackenzie, "*Répertoire international de littérature musicale* (RILM): Immutable Mission amidst Continual Change," in *Music, Libraries, and the Academy: Essays in Honor of Lenore Coral*, ed. by James P. Cassaro, 129–42 (Middleton, Wisc.: A-R Editions, 2007). See also "RILM at 40: A View from the Bridge," *Fontes Artis Musicae* 54, no. 4 (Oct.–Dec. 2007): 421–39.

78. "RIPM: Online Archive of Music Periodicals (1800–1950)," *Fontes Artis Musicae* 54, no.4 (Oct.–Dec. 2007): 391–420.

79. For an informative and entertaining discussion of composition awards, see Adam Silverman, "Keep Your Ears on the Prize: A Hyperhistory of American Composition

Awards," NewMusicBox (1 June 2000), http://www.newmusicbox.org/page.
nmbx?id=14tp00.

80. For more on this award, see Karen R. Little and Julia Graepel, *Grawemeyer Award for Music Composition: The First Twenty Years*, Music Library Association Index and Bibliography Series, 33 (Lanham, Md.: Scarecrow, for the Music Library Association, 2007).

81. Donald W. Krummel, "Observations on Library Acquisitions of Music," *Notes* 23, no. 1 (Sept. 1966): 8.

82. Another disclosure: I was editor of the MLA Technical Reports series when this glossary was published, and my fingerprints are all over the definitions.

Printed in the United States
207288BV00001B/238-315/P